The Warrior's Silence

Ord Elliott

Lightning House
ISBN: 97809858747-4-2 (paperback)
ISBN: 97809858747-6-6 (ebook)

Printed in the United States of America

Book Design: Dotti Albertine

In Memory of Dave Hackett

Dave was my hero, my college friend, my warrior comrade. He was killed in a firefight in the hills above Khe Sanh, Vietnam when he put his own life on the line to save other Marines. He took his last breath next to me. I will always miss him.

About the Book

A veteran retraces his footsteps as a Marine platoon commander in Vietnam. Ord Elliott goes on to reflect on that war and the recent conflicts in Iraq and Afghanistan. He digs deep to confront the emotions that underlie his experience of combat, and with each battle deals with his emerging understanding of war and of the warriors that marched with him—back then and today. Bold, honest, and often heart-rending, this book will speak to his generation and those that have followed.

CONTENTS

ix   *Foreword*

xi   *Preface*

PART I: **Going In — 1964-1969**

1   Princeton University

3   Career Decision

4   Rugby

5   Sophomore Year Marine PLCs

7   Junior Year PLCs

10   Europe

11   Doug

12   Before Leaving

13   Leaving D.C.

14   Arriving in Country

17   Lone Duck

19   Moving Out

22   Okinawa

25   Heading Back

26   Back in Country

29   Khe Sanh

31   Dave

33 M-16s

34 Rituals

35 Breaking the Perimeter

38 The Numbers Game

40 Ambush

42 Out of the Hills

43 The Tripoli

44 Going Back In

47 The Dilemma

50 Pappy Leaves

51 Hammered

53 The March South

55 In the Rear

57 Back Again

59 The Crater

60 Yokosuka

62 On the Way Back

63 Back to D.C.

64 The Job

65 The Protests

67 Checking Out

Getting the Inside Out — 1972

70 "The Drum"

72 "Journal from the Other World"

PART II: Looking Back — 2012

75 The Urge and the Emptiness

76 Forgotten Premonition

77 The Dream

78 The Officers' Reunion

79 *Dateline* Finds Us

81   Reunion for the Troops
82   Wayne's Story
83   My Radio Operator
85   The M-16 Jam Revealed
86   Guillian-Barré
88   Lawrence Livermore Lab
89   Vietnam Redux
91   The March to Bagdad
92   Taking Pfc. Chance
93   McNamara on Point
94   Al Leaves Us
94   Accidental Guerilla
95   Ho Chi Minh
96   We Give Them Names
97   Mothers at the Front
98   Thank You for Your Service
99   Fighting for Your Team
100 But Not for My Daughter
101 The Dalai Lama
101 War Is a Choice
102 Playing Chess
105 Fingers in the Dyke
106 There Will Always Be War
107 Twins
108 The Warrior's Silence

111 *About the Author*

Foreword

Ord Elliott and I played rugby together at Princeton for four seasons. During the last two he was my Captain. In those days the Captain was also the playing coach, and Ord excelled at organizing efficient practices. After his Marine training over the summer of 1965, he was in such good shape that he could run forever, so those practices were often torture.

We later thanked our Captain because we were always in better shape than our opponents. During games, Ord found his leader's voice to exhort us when we dragged and teach us when we forgot our jobs. We all knew Ord would be a great Marine. We were grateful and relieved when he came back from Vietnam.

Since Ord and I kept up over the years, there were chances for me to ask him about the war, but he didn't want to talk about it. I understood because my father had never discussed with me his combat experiences in World War II. I knew *The Warrior's Silence* was the right title for the book. I've been honored to help Ord shape and edit his words. I knew when he showed me his 1978 memoir, as well as the pieces he'd recently set down, that this book had to be published.

It must be read widely, both by veterans of Vietnam and other wars, and by those of us who haven't been in combat—*especially* those of us who haven't been warriors. This superb book helps us understand the emotions veterans bring home and does so by means of its honesty, vivid storytelling, and bold, lucid style.

As I join you in reading *The Warrior's Silence*, I thank my old friend Ord Elliott for once again putting his life on the line—"on point"—and for finding the words to say what cannot be said.

—John Faggi

Preface

In 1978, ten years after my return from Vietnam, I felt such an all-consuming need to write that I quit my teaching job. I figured I had saved enough money to last half a year without working. I bought an old-fashioned, well-used manual typewriter. Before long, the words and paragraphs started rolling out. I had to get it all out. Then, I could move on with my life.

When I was finished, I put the manuscript in the back of my closet. It's been in the back of several closets since then. Over more than three decades, I've felt ambivalent about bringing my story out into the open. Inevitably I decided that this was a part of my life I wanted to keep to myself.

Watching young men and women endure combat in Iraq and Afghanistan changed my mind. I've had time recently to reflect on the war back then—my war—and the wars today. What follows is how I see war and the warrior—then and now.

PART I

Going In

1964-1969

Princeton University

I WAS SITTING ON top of an old standup piano, my head just below the even layer of smoke that hung at an almost perfect altitude three feet below the ceiling. The piano was against the wall in the basement of my club, Tiger Inn. It was a party night. I was watching all the dancing couples immediately in front of me. I was smashed. It was that beautiful numb feeling you sometimes get with just the right amount of beer and scotch—like floating gracefully just below the clouds. Oh, yes, that delicious experience of being part of it all yet apart—a few feet above the dancers, like a ghost. I remember thinking that it was a little parasitic: I was getting just as much enjoyment from all those people sweating with that pulsating, blaring band as they were and without the effort.

Every now and then I'd feel a thread of isolation. Usually, I needed another beer to maintain just the right buzz in my head. At that stage of the evening, there was generally a lady wandering around needing almost any male to dance with, her friend busy with one of several other pastimes that were part of the party weekend ritual at Tiger Inn. So we'd dance one. I'd get a good whiff of her perfume mixed with that special odor of wool and sweat. Then I'd get two more beers, one to chug immediately and one to take back to my perch on the piano.

I was a senior. It was fall, 1965, and I was convinced that I had it all figured out—at least for that year. I didn't fantasize greatly beyond the reality of the present environment. I had beaten the system. I even had a key to the gym so I could sneak into the freshman mixers and snake off with some unsuspecting freshman from Vassar. I worked on being bold. The bottle and the circus effect of the parties were key aids. It was simply easier to jump off the piano and be bizarre than to be cool.

I used to pull ridiculous, absurd pranks with my friends, but I wasn't aware of being extreme. Pulling pranks was exposure. It was easy. I didn't have to really interact. It also insured partial maintenance of my reputation as being wild and a little crazy. At that time, there were simply two kinds of activity—detachment and the absurd performance. I found both amusing.

Absurdity was the ultimate theory of-it-all then. I'm not sure exactly how the theory emerged. All I remember is that it was there, fairly well developed by senior year, and something that I'd bandy about with friends—usually with a rebellious glimmer in my eye, a kind of James Dean approach to pronouncing "it-all." No doubt the existential writers influenced me—such as the terror of being trapped in a monotonous never-ending reality from Sartre's *No Exit* and the scream of defiance from the window at the end of Kafka's *The Trial*. *Waiting for Godot* strikes me as synthesizing the major metaphors of that theory—fears of entrapment, bold defiance, and the ability and joy of being able to laugh at it all. Absurdity was my theology, although I don't remember any need to have a theology.

Within the theory, detachment was still the overriding tactic for survival. Being up on the piano relieved me of the burden of relating. It allowed me to float above it all—and just watch, just a ghost.

world. It was almost adult. It was a business. And since we had achieved the worst year in the history of the team the year before, two wins and something like fourteen losses, it was obviously a challenge to resurrect at least a winning season.

In rugby, injuries were generally to be overcome by ignoring the pain. I was knocked out in one game, left it temporarily to get stitches sewn above my eye, then returned to the game. The next day I separated my shoulder, but two weeks later I was back in the fray. I hated injuries because they kept me away from the action; they gave the tension time to build. I could always feel the muscles tighten in my stomach.

When senior year ended, the rugby team was one of the most difficult aspects of Princeton to leave. It was a creative activity in community with others as much as it was preparation for the hardened facade that was needed to survive in the Marines—the next life phase. I felt I had improved an organization and left it better able to run, perhaps without me at this stage.

All the while, something quiet and protective was falling away. Detachment was no longer a prerogative, not a foolproof scheme to avoid the unpleasantries of the world. One could not entirely escape the infringement of external forces. I remember thinking how I would miss my perch up on the piano, whether it was at a literal piano or on the rugby field. It felt as though both were being pulled from underneath me.

Sophomore Marine PLCs

THE SUMMER OF 1964 was the third year I had been teaching tennis at a boys' camp in Lake Forest. I didn't like teaching tennis much. But there was time to read during the day and it was outside in the sun. Because I worked mostly alone, with only the young boys to talk to, boredom had set in deeply by this third summer. It was only a six- or seven-week affair, leaving plenty of time to finish off the summer at Quantico, Virginia as an officer candidate for the

United States Marine Corps. I had just finished my sophomore year at Princeton and decided on English as my major.

Seconds after I arrived at Quantico, the sergeant whom I had checked in with became very gruff and had me at attention on the porch in front of the building. I stayed that way for three hours. Several other unlucky early arrivers joined me until enough of us were there to fill a large van with wooden benches—affectionately termed a "cattle car"—which transported us another half hour into the wilderness to a desolate camp of Quonset huts, lightweight prefabricated buildings of corrugated steel. This was home for six more weeks. The ride had been a soothing anecdote to the harsh greeting. It was comforting to just be part of the herd.

We were divided into platoons and marched into a larger Quonset where we hurriedly found boots, fatigues, belts, and helmets. The whole set of paraphernalia all smelled new and fit like bags instead of the close-fitting, neatly starched utilities of our slow-speaking Southern drill sergeant. Then went all the hair in broad strokes of the electric razor, gone in only seconds, and then all of us were in formation in gloppy green cotton utilities with blisters already working in those all too new boots—a great sea of skin-colored heads. We were termed "maggots" and "turds" and other sundries by the drill sergeant. Every now and then, someone would chuckle and we'd all be down for twenty pushups or so. It was just a slight reversal of roles already played out earlier in this same summer. Now, *I* was the camper.

The basic activity performed in a variety of ways was to do whatever it was in unison, quickly, and sharply. The D.I., or Drill Instructor, would come in just after lights out, throw on the switch, and have us jump in and out of the racks (bunk beds), coming quickly to attention. "Get in'm... get out of'm... get in'm... get out of'm," he would slowly and deeply growl. Meanwhile, forty-five or so bodies would be flying from bed to floor with the top bunk partner often careening onto the back of his buddy below.

As I jumped about the sixth or seventh time, the rack collapsed and I fell, mattress and metal with me, to the floor. My head was bleeding.

The D.I. was unfazed. "Are you alive, candidate?" he growled, slowly and surely.

"Yes, sir," I replied as deeply voiced as I could.

"Then get your rack together and get in it, candidate," he uttered dryly, turning simultaneously and sharply as he exited the platoon hut for the night. We were even. The game was not to be unnerved by accident or injury. The D.I. had remained hard, impassionate. I had taken my knock in stride. The blood dried quickly.

I would go to sleep almost instantly each night from exhaustion. It seemed always as if the second after I closed my eyes, the lights would blare on with the sky still pitch black outside and the D.I. growling, "Get out of'm, you maggots." The game was amusing and I was usually successful. There was no time for solitude or thought, though we were always cleaning or polishing something. There was no piano to sit on and watch, except the two or three Saturdays we had off to escape to D.C. and civilization. Then I could be the tough Marine. After all, you needed civilians to look down on.

Out in the woods, it was all the same. Everyone was changing and it was difficult to notice any differences. But on the outside, I began feeling better than people. They couldn't get through that obstacle course, most of them, and though it was difficult for me at first, I had now come to enjoy it. My body was getting bigger. I had wanted that for years, having always been thinner than my peers. I couldn't deny that I liked the new muscles and weight.

Junior Year PLCs

NEARLY EVERYONE MADE IT through the first summer at Quantico. It was not an elimination event. Then came the second summer where we were assured that less than half of us would make it to the end. This year I was ready. I was bigger, tougher, had played rugby all year, and knew that I would be the team captain the following fall. I wasn't an old salt but I was saltier and confident. I loved the romantic concept of the soldier of fortune, the warrior who accepts the reality of battle and death. There was no need to question the correctness of the warrior's role. It was its own justification. It was terribly romantic, though I'm sure I did not think of it then in those terms. I accepted the model because there was a history of warriors in my family who were revered. It seemed only natural to accept the path.

I liked pretending I was John Wayne, chinstrap unbuckled on my helmet, charging big-chested into the enemy lines. I was deeply into it that summer. Playing squad leader one day I gave the deep guttural, "Follow me, men," to my squad right as I tripped flat on my face on a piece of barbed wire. Everyone laughed, as did I. It was all part of the drama. There were only blank bullets to face. It was mostly fun. If you were athletic, you made it through. If you couldn't keep up on the "hill trail" and got heat stroke more than once, that was usually it, you were out. The racks would start to empty out. You'd hear the D.I. tell someone to fall out of ranks and pack up, and when you got back from chow, he was gone. We'd have to change bunks, moving into a tighter group as the rows of empty bunks kept increasing. By the end of the summer most of them were empty. We were the elite. The rest were "sent home to their mother."

I remember the pugil sticks. They were rifle length clubs with pads at either end. We wore football helmets and learned how to simulate attacking with bayonets fixed to our rifles. We would beat the hell out of each other. The platoon contests were the most rugged, as selected gladiators would go out into the center to fight for the glory of "your" platoon. I remember taking on this tall gawky guy. He nearly knocked me unconscious until, my arms nearly frozen with fatigue, I was lucky enough to get him solidly on the side of the head. It was a great feeling to watch him fall after the solid, putty-like sound of contact. And, then, there were cheers instead of me taking a shameful beating.

In training we were told our job was to kill whoever the President told us to kill. It was very simple. We simply accepted the warrior's code. We were not taught how to defend ourselves from attacks. Our hand-to-hand combat and pugil stick training had only offensive moves. It was not our job to disarm. It was our job to kill. Every move was efficiently channeled to that glorious goal.

I remember finishing one of those Saturday morning forced marches with heat cramps. Every time I tried to move a muscle it would cramp. If it wasn't intermittently painful I would have just laughed, but when I laughed I got stomach cramps. There were others near me that had heat stroke, a more serious situation in which the body temperature rises and bakes the brain. They were lying semi-conscious on beds of ice cubes designed to bring their body temperature down and prevent them from becoming vegetables or dying, which usually happened to somebody every summer in that muggy Virginia heat. I liked just sitting there, drinking salt water—that being the remedy for heat cramps. It was that drifty feeling like being on the piano and watching it all and not having to go anywhere or be anything—just a set of eyes.

That mellow feeling was always preceded, however, by the kind of physical exercise that brings one to near nausea, that moment when the body wants to collapse and you want to get out of it. I noticed at these times how my thoughts became gloomy. It should have been a premonition. Mostly I noticed how mellow I felt afterwards with time to sit, or even better with that lovely buzz that comes after half a dozen drinks.

Before the end of summer training, we were taken to the ceremonial Marine headquarters, the home of the commandant and the Marine band. Each week they would perform a twilight parade that included an incredible display of marching and hurling of rifles with flashing fixed bayonets. It was the essence of being a Marine. It was a ritual of men in precise synchronous movement. It was an experience that lifted my emotions close to tears in its beauty. It was the reward for the nausea in training. It was the glory of the professional warrior.

I would sometimes feel this beauty when we ran as a platoon. We would chant, respond in unison to the D.I.'s cantations. It was like being propelled in the body of some giant animal. It was bigger, much bigger than myself. It was easier to run with the animal chanting. It was not even like running. You were part of something larger. You were gloriously lost within it. It was quiet inside, moving to the drone of the chanting. It was somewhat like being on the piano. You were in it, but you were also just watching it all without effort.

Europe

I FLEW TO EUROPE for my twenty-first birthday. It was the middle of the summer. The training had just ended and I was on my way to see Danny, my buddy from Wisconsin, and the lake where I had spent my summers for the last ten years. He met me at the airport with a Land Rover, our transportation for this tour. I had almost no hair. I wore Bermuda shorts, white socks, loafers, and a madras shirt—any of which were dead giveaways for an American at the time. I was also a rock. There wasn't anything on me that wasn't muscle. We took off the canvas cover of the Land Rover, wore these Australian military hats, and drove through the French countryside pretending to be the conquering Allied army. We were usually drunk by noon.

After a few weeks, I tired of the movement and longed to be back at the lake where I could sail and play tennis. I was feeling uprooted. There was too much traveling, too many towns and mountains, and the bars became all the same. I needed my perch. I went home early and melted quietly into the known patterns of lake life. My last year at Princeton was soon to arrive.

There were several of us headed into the Marines after graduation at Princeton, including one of my roommates, Randy, and a close friend on the rugby team, John. It was back to Quantico for four months of further training, only this time as second lieutenants with captains as platoon leaders instead of drill sergeants. There was little of the old harassment that had made PLCs amusing. There was more of a work focus, things to be learned so that we would be ready to take a rifle platoon into combat. Vietnam was blazing away. It was the summer of 1966. Yet the prevailing atmosphere was much like college, most of us being fresh graduates. There were friends from school and earlier summers at Quantico. It was an easy transition.

The John Wayne element was ever present as we laughed hilariously at our melodramatic feats within the structure of routine training. Randy would read an excerpt from *Catch 22* nearly every day, and we would reminisce in the bar about the usual mélange of idiotic experiences that must accompany any military organization. The increasing war consciousness only added to the countering humor of our daily experiences.

Doug

I HAD MADE SEVERAL new friends at Quantico. Doug was one of them. We became very close and often went to D.C. on liberty together, when the Marines doled out a few days of free time. My mother had returned to Washington, giving us a convenient place to pass out after the normal drunken night in Georgetown. One weekend I returned to Princeton to party and see friends. I noticed a difference. I felt apart. I found my old perch on the piano but it wasn't the same. There was no longer that lost feeling. It would never be the reclusive hideout it had been.

Amidst the beer and dancing, I was called for an emergency phone message. It was John. My friend Doug had been in a car accident. They didn't think he would live. He was unconscious. I drove four hours to Bethesda Naval Hospital and saw Doug in intensive care, just a body breathing in spurts. The next morning Doug died.

I was crying as I packed his gear. Since we were so close, I had been asked to take his body back to Lincoln, Nebraska where he had lived with his grandmother. I watched as the makeup was applied to his lifeless body. The corpsman who had prepared his body talked mechanically about his work. Doug's eyes and femurs were taken out and given to the hospital. His mouth was wired shut. I helped put the Marine Corps dress blues on his body, fighting the tears. It brought a change in me. I was quieter. I didn't feel like John Wayne or like playing John Wayne. Doug and I had been jovial actors of that drama. It was dead. It died with Doug.

Before Leaving

THE REAL DRAMA WAS suddenly becoming more real. We were all trained to become rifle platoon leaders. Not everyone wanted that job, but it was considered to be the essence of being a Marine— "the queen of the Marines," as our platoon commander referred to the infantry. Enough of us sought the infantry—the right to lead forty-four enlisted Marines—that there was competition. I wanted it badly, along with orders to Vietnam. After all, that's what it was all about.

Most of us got both. The fighting had picked up. They were starting to lose lieutenants with greater regularity. It was the most dangerous job in the field. You were the leader. You were always a target for snipers. But we had been well trained. The warrior's code was strong in us. We cheered with enthusiasm as one by one, so many of us were chosen for the queen, and also chosen to go "across the big pond," as the phrase went. We were going to war. We were ready, the whole fraternity of us.

Nearly ninety of us were to leave in mid-January. It was just about Thanksgiving when the training ended. We took the month and a half that was allotted to us for leave before the crossing. We took two months' advance pay. We said goodbye to those who weren't going immediately. We knew the odds. Eight out of ten would get the Purple Heart—four seriously wounded and four fatally. It was the supreme test, to be under fire. We would be real warriors soon. We would not all see each other again.

I took several trips to New York City. I spent money, saw friends, and got very smashed. Two worlds seemed to be splitting apart as if some giant earthquake were dividing the earth. There were my friends still in school or going to graduate school, and there was this great war vessel for which I was about to leave. Most of us on the vessel were split apart, at home seeing family before the voyage. I felt a sensation of isolation that was new. There was no club, no group in this interim period. I wouldn't be going to a platoon of my peers but mostly younger, enlisted Marines.

Leaving D.C.

I LEFT D.C. SHORTLY after Christmas. I said goodbye to my mother and grandmother. I remember my mother seeing me off from the steps of her Georgetown apartment. We just looked at each other. There was nothing to say. I left for California, joining my father and a large family contingent to watch Purdue play U.S.C. in the Rose Bowl. I was also on the West Coast because I would leave from there to Vietnam. The contrasting reasons seemed incongruous to me.

My friend Danny, from Wisconsin, and I had started a fat race. We were both tipping the scales at 190 pounds or so. We decided it would be amusing to see who could get to 220 first before the end of the holidays. After all, eating and drinking were the main events. I had to buy a new pair of pants to accommodate my expanding waist. I wore them every day. I got to 217. Danny won, though, and kept on gaining for several more months. I knew it was going to change quickly for me. I had seen the skeletal figures of returning Marine infantrymen.

I was to report that afternoon to Staging Battalion at Camp Pendleton. The troops were being given last minute special training to prepare them for Vietnam. The officers wandered around watching or semi-participating to kill time. The waiting was uncomfortable. I remember a salty gunnery sergeant starting his warning—full oration to the troops with, "There's only two ways you're gonna come back, Marine—intact or tacked in." I felt irritated at the unnecessary scare. The whole play was becoming all too real. Pendleton was a nomad's land. It was a foggy wasteland between two worlds separated more by the inevitability of time than by distance.

I spent the last weekend in San Diego. I went to the Friday night happy hour at the Marine Corps Recruit Depot—a regular for hoards of drunken Marine and Navy officers and any babe who had the courage to come in. Drinks were about 10 cents each. Everyone was bombed. Some lady dragged me into the women's john with her. The whole evening was hilarious, the biggest body exchange I had ever seen.

I didn't want to leave the balmy Southern California reality. I remember spending the last morning looking out at the still seas. I remember the emptiness of the beach. I felt a sense of quiet around me. I was aware of being alone in that veil. I drove back to Pendleton that evening in a heavy fog. The next day was Sunday, January 15, 1967. It was the day of the first Super Bowl. I missed the game. I left with a planeload of Marines for Okinawa, the first stop on the way across the big pond.

We stopped for gas on Wake Island. Some Marine had missed his birthday in crossing the International Date Line. We were in the air for almost a day traveling on a military plane with canvas strapped seats. The wires and pipes all showed like a skeletal X-ray. We all wore green. We were in Okinawa for only a few days, but it seemed long. There was time to mail letters, to think. I lived in spartan but pleasant officers' quarters. Our clothes were cleaned every day by the friendly and incredibly hard-working Japanese women. The food was plentiful. There was time to read. I was engrossed in *Atlas Shrugged*. The night before I left, I watched some major pick my book off the hat-shelf where I would leave it during dinner and walk off. I was two-thirds through. I was angry. I thought of stopping him, but it didn't seem worth the confrontation. I wasn't planning to take any books to Vietnam. I watched the sunset instead, the most gorgeous, red, glowing sunset I had ever seen. I felt sad and distant.

Word had reached us in Okinawa that one of our second lieutenant buddies from Quantico who had only left a few days earlier had "bought the farm"—shot in the head by a sniper his first day out. This was not reassuring. I left on a plane of mostly officers for Da Nang, a Continental Airlines flight. There were stewardesses. We had the usual airline meal. Everyone wore green except the stewardesses, who had on their customary outfits. It seemed bizarre. We knew the plane would be shot at by the Viet Cong as we flew into Da Nang. Just before we had left, a saltier captain had commented while surveying this large plane-size group that a lot of us would not be coming back. I had been thinking about myself and my friends. I remember looking around slowly at everyone. I decided that I was coming back.

Arriving in Country

THE STEWARDESSES GAVE US warm, maternal looks of good-bye as we left the plane. "We'll see you!" they said, optimistically. Their eyes said that they knew it would not be that way. Civilization disappeared at the door of the plane. I was in Da Nang. You could hear the artillery. You could hear the roar of Marine Phantoms, supersonic fighter jets, taking off and landing. It was night—black, misty, and muddy. I felt greasy, unshaven, tired, and uncomfortable. We spent the night huddled under a large tarp since it was too late to assign us bunks. Some drunken sergeant in charge of the transit process blared over the microphone for an hour, mostly bellowing unnecessary information designed to intimidate new arrivals. It was perverse. Finally there was just the sound of the artillery and the planes. Once in a while you could hear small arms fire in the distant hills. The Viet Cong, "Gooks" we called them, were only a few miles away.

The next morning, assignments were made to regiments. I was flown north from Da Nang to Dong Ha to join the Third Marines Division. I was driven in a Jeep along a broken dirt road west to

Camp Carroll, a Marine base that rested on a plateau just below the demilitarized zone. It was my first taste of the Vietnamese population, driving through the rice paddies and through a few villages where people sold food and moved peacefully between thatched huts. There was no civilian population north of this highway—the northernmost line of the U.S. defense. The area was bucolic. It smelled different. It seemed strange to have a war in such a lovely country. I didn't really want to be there. I remember thinking that I was there because of my own decisions and actions; I was halfway around the world. Part of me wanted to take it all back.

I was assigned as platoon leader of the First Platoon, Hotel Company, Second Battalion, Third Marines. Camp Carroll was the battalion's home. Lt. Col. Ohanesian was the battalion CO, or Commanding Officer. Ohanesian was a friend of my Marine uncle—Col. James Ord. My uncle had been a Marine rifle platoon commander on Iwo Jima, a company commander in Korea, and would later become a regimental commander in Vietnam. Uncle Jimmy was like a father to me and no doubt a huge factor in me becoming a Marine. I had met Ohanesian while I was still in college. He was a tall, big, strong, confident-looking man. He had a gentle, quiet way about him. I was glad to be in his battalion. A friend from Princeton, Dave Hackett, was the second platoon leader in my company. He had graduated a year earlier than I from school. He had been captain of the soccer team. He had already been in Vietnam half a year. He had tasted combat. I was reassured to have friends near me.

It was muddy and misty most of the time—it was the end of monsoon season. The Tet (Vietnamese) New Year was approaching. I wrote to my mother that the food was good and that I lived in a large tent with two of my sergeants, both black, who owned a small portable record player. They'd do their jiving in the tent at night and get me laughing and forgetting for the moment where I was. The nights were surprisingly cold. We had cots and blankets. The army had two gigantic 175-mm guns about fifty feet away which shot intermittently over our heads all night long. I had one squad on the camp's perimeter and two on separate knolls to the north. At least one of them was out on patrol each night. Some days I was very busy while on other days there was nothing to do. I hadn't gotten any mail since I'd left the States.

My Marine uncle, Colonel James B. Ord

Lone Duck

I'D BEEN IN COUNTRY less than two weeks when my first test as a green lieutenant came. My platoon was to be helicoptered north to spend a week searching for infiltration routes. We were to sit on a hill and run patrols at night during the Tet New Year. There might be no one in the hills or there might be a whole division of North Vietnamese Regulars, the only enemy this far north. The VC were scarecrows in comparison.

As it turned out we never sat still. We moved during the day as a platoon and sent out squad patrols at night. It was a grueling pace.

I began to get the concept of the tactic. We were a decoy. We were out there to fix the location of the NVA. If we got wiped out because we ran into a regiment, that was all part of the game. Then the battalion would mass larger forces, no loss to them. Our code name was "Lone Duck."

I came to realize that I was well trained. I knew my way in the thick canopy and mountains. I could read maps, set my platoon in tight defensive positions, chart patrol routes, but there were still frustrations. As I was settling my platoon in at dusk one evening, word came that I had to move another thousand meters west. We had already cut our way through the elephant grass to get on this knoll. The Division HQ had planned harassment and interdiction artillery fire on my spot and wanted me to move. Lazy bastards, I thought. Was it that much trouble to change the target location? I estimated that it would take at least several hours to hack our way through the thick, ten-foot elephant grass to the new position. Some colonel barked at me that he was looking at a map and that it should only be knee-high grass along my route. Perhaps I was lost, he suggested. I knew where I was. I also knew that the maps were crafted mostly by the French about twenty years earlier, and only an idiot would look at a map and determine on that basis alone the exact nature of the terrain. In short, I was talking to some field-grade moron who, back in his tent, was moving pins on his map like some kind of Monopoly game.

We were ordered to move, over my protests. Half an hour later, we had hacked our way about fifty meters. It was dark. We were ordered back up on the knoll we had just left. My men were grumbling in the dark—exhausted, frustrated. They needed to be quiet, especially at this time of day when voices carried like shots for miles, giving our position away. But I couldn't blame them; they had seen this idiotic kind of maneuver before. Each day brought them only another brand of suffering. John Wayne wasn't in Vietnam. He was in Hollywood.

And yet I was disappointed that I had not tasted my first firefight, thinking of myself as still green until I had been shot at. There was a reconnaissance unit that got into it north of us, but they were too far away for us to help. Still, I came back to camp confident that I knew my business. I knew the hills north of the camp as well. Thousands of men could be swallowed on the side of a hill. I wished we could move more quietly, more surreptitiously. There was always the noise of a resupply helicopter announcing our arrival. To make matters worse, the Marines insisted on camping on top of hills, making our presence well known to any pair of eyes within miles. That was what our senior officers wanted, I suppose. Yet, I wanted to be the watcher—hidden, invisible on the piano—just a part of it all.

Camped with my platoon searching for the NVA

Moving Out

OUR BATTALION HAD A new mission. We were being sent to Okinawa for a month to train and reorganize for floating duty. We would be put on ships off the coast of Vietnam as a movable strike force, termed SLF or special landing force. Before the battalion was to move, our company was to march south into the Ba Long Valley and exchange places with another of the battalion's companies. It was a lovely two-day march. The valley was V-shaped at the camp-site with high rugged mountains, all moving symmetrically into the vortex. There was a South Vietnamese unit in the valley as well. You could smell the dried fish sauce that was their staple additive to rice. There was a river running alongside the camp, and I had my first bath in a month. It was high living.

My Marines got lazy. I caught several asleep on post at night. It was understandable. We never really slept for any length of time in the field. We were up on watch, then sleeping lightly for a few hours at most, then watch. The platoon sergeant and I took turns. On our watch we would move quietly from foxhole to foxhole along our lines in the pitch black. Companies had been assaulted and wiped out because of sleeping Marines. There were numerous options to maintain discipline, to keep the men awake. The sergeants tended to prefer a swift kick in the sleeping Marine's head. Most officers either chewed their men out or initiated administrative or judicial punishment. I didn't like either. I made them write one thousand word essays on how they would feel if their sleeping caused the death of all their buddies. They hated it. Most of them could hardly write. Every other word in their papers was some sort of profanity. They were hilarious and effective—one essay seemed to do it. I never caught the same Marine asleep again. One night I feel asleep on my watch. My platoon sergeant and right guide had a big snicker the next morning. I was glad I had never clobbered one of my men asleep on post.

Camp Carroll was shelled while we were in Ba Long. Colonel Ohanesian took two companies into the field almost at once. They moved in a long column north and were ambushed. The Colonel was shot in both legs. Then they were mortared. The Sergeant Major lost both hands. They were pinned down, with no chance for medevac helicopters to get in. The Colonel died quietly in the night. He had lost too much blood. The Sergeant Major bled to death as well. At least thirty other Marines were killed, and a hundred were wounded.

We heard it, bits and pieces, over the radio. We were waiting for orders that would bring us north, but they never came. The fighting finally subsided enough to allow withdrawal, and another battalion was brought into action. We were helilifted back to Dong Ha to be transported with the rest of the battalion by boat to Okinawa as planned. We watched the landing pad at Dong Ha as the dead and wounded were brought in with regularity. We were like a pack of crows, hovering over the slaughtered, eager to see who would be brought in next.

The remaining members of the company were reunited. As we climbed aboard a troop ship that would steam us to Okinawa, the Captain played a record over the loudspeaker. There were several songs. I only remember "The Yellow Rose of Texas." It was a jubilant, welcome-home-hero feeling. I felt a new sense of safety, of relaxation. It was different when you didn't have to worry about being shot at.

We had a new battalion commander, Lt. Col. DeLong, or "Pappy," as he was called. I had met him once just after arriving in Dong Ha. He looked me coldly in the eye then and said, "You'll be getting bloodied soon, lieutenant," as though that ought to delight me. I tightened up immediately. He had commanded another battalion in the regiment. They had fought a major battle along Mudder's Ridge, and had had the hell bombed out of them. They were known for being well dug-in. Pappy was tough but respected.

He was the last one aboard ship. He called all the officers and staff non-commissioned officers on deck. He chewed us out for getting wiped by the North Vietnamese Army at Camp Carroll. We were lazy, undisciplined. We'd run a sloppy operation, and gotten our just desserts. From now on we'd be properly defended, and that meant digging deep foxholes that were well-sandbagged. We'd wear flak jackets and helmets at all times; everyone would shave every day in the field, even if that meant using a dry razor—there would be no moustaches. The new sergeant major standing next to him had a gorgeous moustache. It was gone an hour later. Pappy exited the deck first with the same scowl he had arrived with. Everyone grumbled. He had insulted Col. Ohanesian by berating his tactics—and to what end, since he was dead? Pappy had held us all responsible. I did not find him pleasant. I respected him, nonetheless.

Okinawa

IT WAS A ROUGH ride through the China Sea to Okinawa. I was seasick most of the way. At least I had a quiet bed in the officers' area. My men were stacked seven-high in the front of the ship, vomiting over each other. I had come to care about them very much. They seemed so young. Most of them were eighteen or nineteen-years-old. I was twenty-two. I felt more like their father.

We were based at Camp Schwab, a clean, new-looking concrete set of structures. The officers lived separately on the hill. I had grown accustomed to being with my men, so this separation felt artificial, although relaxing. I could read, throw the football with Dave, jog—it was more like college than Vietnam. There were inspections and formations and all the rinky-dink that goes with military at peace. It was no wonder so many preferred certain less formal aspects of Vietnam.

Dave became the executive officer of the company, as the senior second lieutenant. We got a new company commander and a new lieutenant. I was no longer the greenest. We had a parade and a ceremony for the dead of the company. I have pictures of it all—the lone trumpeter sounding the twilight chords, the rifles with fixed bayonet stuck in the dirt in neat rows, helmets resting on the butts of the rifles—and all of this a symbol for those in the battalion who had given it all up.

The Company First Sergeant was in his second year in Vietnam. He had extended twice. An extension was for six months, entitling you to a month's vacation anywhere in the world before returning to fulfill that obligation. He had refused the vacation. He had refused to go on R-and-R—the several day rest and relaxation period normally granted to each Marine during the thirteen-month Vietnam duty. He always wore his uniform, even on liberty. He refused to wear civilian clothes. He had even brought his dress blues (a formal uniform) with him to Vietnam. His nickname was "Locker Box" Jones, so given because he was renowned for throwing large locker boxes around when disgusted with the troops. He had scars across his face and chest from Korea. He was built like a large rock. He never smiled. He always went into the field with the company rather than staying behind shuffling papers, as was the custom for first sergeants. He was what it meant to be a Marine. He was a living definition of total commitment, not a teller of tall tales or heroic deeds.

Memorial for troops on Okinawa

Near the end of our stay on Okinawa, we went to the Northern Training Area to practice various jungle maneuvers. We noticed a film crew in one of the remote areas staging a helicopter assault. We found out later it was John Wayne filming *The Green Berets*. I was mildly infuriated. I wanted him to do it for real, in Vietnam. I wanted him to land in a real, hot LZ, a bona fide landing zone to face the bullets. What did he know of war, I thought. I had seen the butchered bodies. I had been afraid for real, yet I was still hungry for the excitement of my first firefight, for the real taste of combat, for the assault up the hill into enemy fire. It seemed comical to have

Running my platoon in Okinawa

My platoon on Okinawa before we shipped back to Vietnam

seen him in the flesh for the first time, making a film about the war I was in. I had caught up to him at last.

Heading Back

SEVERAL DAYS LATER, MY platoon was in a tossing landing craft approaching our new floating home. Soon we were climbing the ropes up to the deck of the ship. The ship was a reconditioned World War II aircraft carrier, now designed as a helicopter amphibious assault ship. Ironically, it was named the USS Princeton. The battalion that had been afloat before us enjoyed a calm several-month ride at sea, with sea trips to the Philippines and Taipei for liberty. There were occasional landings and operations, but it was mostly soft duty. There were real beds and showers and excellent food served on white tablecloths in the officers' mess. There was time to read and be with yourself.

The wardroom etiquette book was waiting in our bunkroom. There were three of us in one good-size room for a ship, all second lieutenant platoon commanders for Hotel Company. The guidebook was evidently placed there to remind us rowdy Marines that in the wardroom, we had to behave as politely as our navy counterparts. We had been taught to despise the soft, ill-trained Navy. We were the real warriors. They were lucky enough to have a chance to carry the real heroes in their vessels. We heaped our scorn on the etiquette manual. This "Emily Post" counterfeit was laughable.

We called the Navy men "squids," and we did everything we could to upset our squid counterparts. We talked too loudly, ate too much food at a time, and were obscenely profane. We acted like boisterous aborigines, intent on despoiling the immaculate wardroom. The commodore of the fleet wanted the Marines to wear sneakers instead of combat boots so as not to scratch his pretty decks. It was a war of propriety versus the gruff Marine tour de force. The commodore wanted to emasculate us by taking our boots. But Pappy was firm. We wore our boots. He would not have his Marines humiliated.

We, in turn, had come to respect his hard-headed discipline. This was the single thread that separated Marines from everyone else. You would give due credit to the enemy if they were disciplined, but these Navy debutantes were not deserving.

Back in Country

IT WAS NOT LONG before we were again traveling off the coast of Vietnam. The blue seas and sky were beautiful against the sandy shores eight miles off. It was a peaceful, idyllic feeling. An assault had been planned south of Quang Tri in the I Corps region. This was about twenty miles south of Da Nang. Here there were Viet Cong and booby traps and the North Vietnamese Army farther north—it was not like nomad's land.

It was just like in the movies: we waited quietly just off the main deck 'til the blowing pipes signaled to load. We raced in neat columns into the waiting CH-46 helicopters and took off quietly in formation. You never felt as though you were lifting off in a helicopter. The boat just seemed to get further away. Then came the beautiful ride in the sky, the regular drone of the turbine-powered, twin-bladed chopper, the approaching land, the quiet; then the transition from the romance of the spectacular Hollywood take-off to the stillness inside as you realized that death was at the doorstep again. We landed without opposition on a ridge of sand dunes. As the helicopters left, I always felt the isolation: the great machines of civilization left us only our feet in the dirt—we were animals again in the heat, worrying about quenching our thirst while the Navy sipped Cokes safely offshore.

We wandered, our whole company, through the sand and past desolate villages some ten miles inland. Suddenly, there was an explosion. One man died almost instantly from a booby-trapped tree—and then the quiet. We were back at war. My sixth sense was in operation again, seeing possible ambush sites, always hypothesizing how I would maneuver my men if we got hit here or there.

The first landing in Quang Tri

A break with my radio operator, David

The next day we moved in with the battalion. Pappy sent for me. My platoon was going to check out a village on the coast. Intelligence had reported VC in that area. Pappy was tough but paternal, like his nickname. You knew he loved his Marines. Having your mission given by Pappy instead of the company commander gave you a feeling of special importance. He was comforting but challenging. "Come back safe, but go get those bloody Gooks!" he would say. It was that dual aspect of character that made him one of the great combat leaders. He was tough, ready to die, ready for you to die, but his caring was strong. You would fight for him.

There was no one in the village except a few old men and women, and a few younger children. It was so tranquil along the coast. The poor village with its thatched huts was a cool contrast to the hot, barren sands we had pulled our heavily loaded, sweating bodies through. An old Vietnamese man gave me a cup of water. He sat quietly and smiled. Perhaps he was just glad we did not burn his home. I just wanted to sit along the beach—I didn't like being at war. This movement through the sand to hills named by their elevations seemed a senseless waste of energy. There had to be better ways to live your life. Just when you had relaxed, the orders came to move. The breeze had cooled my body. I hated to move and feel the cold, moist sweat all over me. The steel helmet and flak jacket made a good oven.

Alone with my platoon, I was roaming past a village filled with flimsy hooch-like huts. Suddenly, the crack of bullets split the air around me. We were instantly on the ground. I moved my men with business-like sureness, pointed my machine gun teams to get cross-fire against the line of trees where we were drawing fire, and brought the rocket launcher up to plaster a hooch with a Willie Peter round (white phosphorous). It was exhilarating. We were in the vast majority. The shots against us were wild, the danger was minimal. I called in a Huey Gunship from the carrier and had the hooch completely blown away. I set a base of fire with one squad and was moving two squads up, fire team by fire team, to get within assault distance. It was a textbook attack. I felt confident. It was almost fun.

Over the radio, I received a strange set of orders from Ray, my company commander, who was with the rest of the company several thousand kilometers away. They were sending helicopters to pick us up. We were not to assault. We would be taken to another location as would the rest of the company. Something more important had emerged. We would be told the details later.

It was bad timing. We were deployed less than a hundred meters from the VC. Withdrawal meant pulling my men out a squad at a time, while under fire. The choppers came, one at a time. Their .50-caliber machine guns blasted the tree line as my Marines filed in. My radio operator, David, and I got on the last chopper with the third squad, but the total weight was too much. We got off with the fire still coming in, hoping for a quick pick-up before the VC noticed just two of us remained. It was a vulnerable feeling thinking we might be forgotten until the next CH-46 helicopter arrived.

But we made it. No one was hurt. It was my first firefight, and it was easy. I was seasoned now. It was like losing your virginity— bound to happen eventually. I was relieved just to have it over with.

Khe Sanh

THE CHOPPERS LANDED AT Da Nang. We boarded C-130 transport planes to fly to Khe Sanh, an outpost of the northwest edge of the DMZ. It was only a few miles to Laos from there. We were given new maps, new codes, and radio channels. It had been quiet up there for a long time, we were told. There was an airfield at Khe Sanh and a Marine rifle company to guard it. A six-man forward observer team had been sent up in the hills and was ambushed. One man made it back alive. They had sent a platoon up. It had been hit hard and was pinned down just below the summit of Hill 861 by at least a company of NVA heavily dug in. We would be on our way up that afternoon.

We were away from the easy game of random shots with the VC. This was more serious. The senior officers had tight, concerned expressions on their faces. They were filling dozens of body bags already at the airfield at Khe Sanh. I heard that the platoon commander pinned down with his men below Hill 861 was a friend from basic training. We had come to Vietnam together. They had gotten out finally with the help of close air support and artillery. He was alive. He had lost his arm. They had rolled grenades down the steep hill on top of his troops.

As we moved north into the hills from the red clay of the airfield, you could smell the stench of rotting dead bodies. I saw a hand lying in the brush with nothing else near it. It seemed insane to be walking into this. Pappy didn't believe in wasting his men senselessly. He had the clout of success on his side. He convinced General Walt to bomb the hell out of 861 before sending more bodies into a heavily fortified position.

Hill 861 getting pounded before we move out

The May 12, 1967 issue of *Time* magazine carried a full story on the battle: "The first hill the Marines charged was 861. They reached the top but could not hold it under heavy fire from the entrenched communists, who refused to break and run as they have so often done in Vietnam once U.S. troops closed with them. The Marines withdrew and let the air and artillery knock off the top of the hill, blasting away foliage and great chunks of earth and rock. After that the Marine tactic became, as Lieut. Col. Gary Wilder explained, 'to use just enough Marines to fix a target, then pull back and use our ordnance.' The lethal rain of ordnance that they called in worked on Hill 861; two days later the Marines took it without difficulty. The enemy dead were larger and better fed than usual, and their uniforms were new khaki or tiger suits. Some even wore steel helmets, and many had been using high-powered sniper rifles with scopes. One battalion of Marines then moved toward Hill 881 South, the other toward 881 North."

Dave

WE WERE THE FIRST company to move north of 861. The terrain was thick, steep, and rugged. We moved slowly and settled on a knoll for the night that was not quite midway between 861 and 881 North. My friend Dave, now the company executive officer, camped with my platoon for the night. We had had many discussions in our time together in Vietnam. Dave was fond of Indian stories and was reading a series of novels on the Old West. The protagonist in this series was a half-white, half-Indian named Big Lou, whom Dave described as strong, wily, tenacious, very courageous, and without fear. Big Lou always commanded his respect. Dave always had mine. Dave would often recount one of Big Lou's most harrowing feats or escapes. He had just finished the last novel in the series before we left the USS Princeton a week earlier. But Dave told me that the invincible Big Lou is finally killed. There was a quiet nostalgia in his voice as he told me this last tale. We drank a cup of coffee silently and peered into the darkening hills. He was a very close friend and companion. He was a good Marine. He never questioned the war much. He was a professional soldier; like Big Lou, he accepted the rules of the game he was in.

The next evening I drank coffee without Dave. He was dead. The second platoon moved out first that morning with their "green" second lieutenant. Dave went with them; my platoon was behind.

They walked into an ambush. A row of machine gun nests had pinned down most of the platoon, while snipers in the trees struck with their deadly scopes. Dave had stood up to see where the fire was coming from. It was a heroic and selfless act to save his fellow Marines. He was shot in the head. We were higher up and managed to get two machine guns in position to rake the NVA line. It was hard to see where they were entrenched although they were less than fifty meters away. Sniper shots made peering dangerous. They pulled Dave back up on the knoll. He was breathing but unconscious. The corpsman (Navy medic) had given him mouth-to-mouth resuscitation to keep him breathing but had given up. It was hopeless.

We were still fighting, trying to get artillery in on the position. Other men were killed and wounded. The second platoon's lieutenant was alive but had been shot in the hip. We were just trying to get our troops out of the crossfire. Dave lived for about ten more minutes, his limp body breathing sporadically. I was a few feet away fighting the battle and fighting my tears. I was angry. I was furious. This stupid war was taking my friend.

The artillery finally started coming in. We had saved most of the second platoon. Dave had stopped breathing. I asked the corpsman the question I already knew the answer to. Dave was quiet, immobile. The firefight was over. The NVA had pulled back, as had we. The medevac helicopters were coming in. We had chopped away enough of a clearing for them to land.

I knew they would put Dave's body in a long plastic bag at the airfield. It would be flown to Saigon's large mortuary. We all knew the procedure. Life seemed so frail, so easily ended. I hated this war, and from that point on, I only cared about keeping myself and my men alive.

We moved back a thousand meters to the battalion CP (command post). Another company's turn had come to take the point. They were advancing up the finger (the ridge) to our right, avoiding the path that led to our ambush, hoping to catch our attackers as they moved north. Pappy had a good sense of the land, how to use it, how to move companies and platoons—leapfrogging, enveloping. He was not one to send his men straight up the hill into fortified positions. He had been a grunt in earlier wars. He knew what it was like to be the point infantryman, often a sacrificial lamb in the initial contact. He knew, too, when a unit had been hit hard and demoralized. He brought us back to him to rebuild our confidence.

Dave (left) and me on Okinawa a month before Dave was killed

M-16s

NEWS OF OUR BATTLE had reached Da Nang. A few of the braver war correspondents and photographers had been allowed to travel to the front. A French female photographer was now at the battalion command post. She was already a seasoned combat veteran, we were told, and she was even allowed to go out with one of the advancing companies. They made quick contact moving slowly up a ridge line.

One squad assaulted an entrenched pocket of NVA. Many of their M-16 rifles jammed—a terrifying problem that was just beginning to occur as we had switched from the heavier but more trustworthy M-14 rifles. The only way to clear the jam was to push a cleaning rod down the barrel to break the cartridge free. This time several Marines were found shot in the head, cleaning rods out, their weapons jammed; helplessly unarmed, they were slaughtered. The French lady was shot in the chest. My mother saw her pictures only a week later in *Life* magazine.

The high command claimed we had not properly kept the weapons cleaned, an assertion we knew was false. The M-16s malfunctioned too often; we had no confidence in them. As an officer, I carried a .45-caliber pistol since it was not my job to shoot but to direct my men and their fire. On this campaign several of the lieutenants, including myself, were carrying shotguns as well, checked out from Special Services. We knew the danger of ambush or being overrun were the only times they were needed. Somehow this operation had kindled our fears. Perhaps not trusting the M-16, which nearly all my men carried, added to this self-preservation instinct.

Rituals

I HAD BECOME AN expert at doctoring up C-rations. I carried a small bottle of dried onions and another of hot sauce. I made a fantasy beef stroganoff by combining chicken and noodles with spiced beef and the onion and hot sauce additives. I served English muffins in the morning by slicing the jarred pieces of bread in half and roasting each portion over the flame of a heat tab, flammable tablets that were our only heat source in the field. In spite of the doctored food, I now wore the smallest-sized utilities, and they still needed to be cinched up in the waist. Usually I just ate one meal a day in the heat. Every now and then, when we were in a more permanent base camp, I would get a box of canned fruit from home. The three types of meals that contained canned fruit were always in high demand. I took mostly fruit on an operation. We carried the cans in a spare pair of socks slung over our ancient World War II knapsack.

Small rituals became important. Pappy made everyone shave every day. I would use a few drops of precious water to brush my teeth and shave each morning. Pappy was right to make us shave— the daily procedure, however bizarre in the jungle, added to a feeling of discipline, and discipline was related to confidence. There was such a thin line between hope and the apathy that was referred to as combat fatigue, a state I had seen some reach when they had just had too much war, and they exuded deadness. It was dangerous to get that way. I had felt the fringes of it already. Sitting on the edge of my foxhole one day, a sniper fired on the platoon. He was far away; several shots flickered nearby. I just sat on the edge of my half-dug foxhole, vulnerable to the sniper's fire, unwilling to go to the discomfort of lying in the mud. It was the first week of May. It had been nearly four months since the first Super Bowl game. That seemed like it was from another lifetime.

Breaking the Perimeter

WE WERE RUNNING LONG patrols up the fingers that led to 881 North. Echo Company was the first to move up the last knoll before the summit. *Time* Magazine continued their account: "The northern peak of 881 proved nearly as difficult for Lieut. Colonel Earl ("Pappy") DeLong's 2nd Battalion. Halfway up the slope, the Marines ran into heavy fire from bunkers, and bedded down. A cold rain blew up during the night, and just before dawn the North Vietnamese came charging down from the summit, penetrating a company perimeter. Jerking on their boots, the Marines repulsed the attackers. But twenty-eight Marines were killed and sixty-one wounded. Once again, the Marines waited and watched while air and artillery slashed at the red bunkers dug in above them, reducing the hilltop to a bare, burnt knob."

This story misses the more sordid reality. Echo Company was

My radio operator, David, and a squad leader in a foxhole on 881

hammered. They were surprised, caught off-guard. They had moved into the NVA bunkers on the hill but had failed to notice another set of bunkers only yards away that skirted the inner perimeter. The NVA had returned after dusk and redeployed around the northwest edge of the Marine line. They broke through the perimeter and raised havoc inside. There was no line of enemy to fire into. Everyone was shooting in nearly every direction. There were dead and dying Marines all over; half the company had been wiped out in only a few minutes. That was the way of war in Vietnam. There were few long sieges, just the sudden burst of fire, the dead, the fallen, then the silence, or the desperate calls for "corpsman."

The NVA were too close for artillery. Echo Company had lost its fighting spirit. It was their turn to be down. Our company was sent up the ridge to the north to envelop. Ray, the captain and company CO, decided to send my platoon through the saddle (the ridge between two peaks) the last hundred meters to the broken Marine lines. We would take the NVA from behind.

We moved quietly into position. I crawled through the brush and peered into the dip in the thick terrain that separated the two hilltops. We fixed bayonets knowing that the M-16s might jam. I decided to put one squad on line and move them through slowly. Another would follow directly behind to counter an ambush from the rear while my machine guns and the third squad deployed as a base of fire to protect the advancing men. I knew what I was doing. I would move with the second squad.

I had sent my best squad down first with two trustworthy corporals who, in peacetime, would have probably still been young privates. The war and the high kill rate for infantry made promotions fast. They were old salts at nineteen-years-old with seven or eight months in the country. They were lucky to still be alive.

The squad moved out. I watched them quickly disappear into the ten-foot-high canopy. I noticed at the edge of the other hill the darkened face of an NVA soldier who had risen from his bunker to listen more intently at whatever noise my Marines were making. David, my radioman who was always with me, took aim before he could spot any of the first squad already on the move. David fired several times and nicked him once. The NVA soldier just peered around apparently unaware of where the shots were coming from. He did not seem concerned.

Moments later, my first squad surprised the entrenched NVA and killed four of them. One of my corporals had jumped into a foxhole and shot an NVA soldier with his pistol. Nearby another NVA soldier leaped from his hole and was about to gun down Roy, one of my riflemen. His M-16 jammed as we feared some of them would. Luckily the fire team leader, Connie, who was nearby, blasted the NVA first. I was just behind with the second squad. By then we had made the link to Echo Company and secured their perimeter. They could bring in the medevac helicopters now and take out the wounded and stacks of dead. The smell made you want to vomit—so many were dead, with time enough to begin rotting in the humidity and heat.

We searched several of the NVA bodies. One was just a boy—he could have been fourteen. In his wallet was fresh North Vietnamese currency. He had a picture of himself with his family—he was standing with his parents and sisters around their dining table. It was a very civilized setting. It was shockingly American in its context. He was so young. I had been teaching boys his age tennis only two years earlier. I could see the tears that would spring from his parents' eyes. The enemy was no longer the enemy. I felt such intense hate for the politicians and generals who sat quietly back and directed us all in this monopoly of death. I wanted those bastards to come and duel each other to the death. Let those who start wars lead the charge. Let them taste their own blood. Let them watch their weakened limbs as life rushes away. Let them rot in the jungle in place of these boys.

We had called in recoilless rifle fire over our position to kill any retreating NVA, the beauty of recoilless rifles being that they were lightweight and fired artillery-type shells at range. I moved from a position I had been standing in for a number of minutes. One of our rounds fell short and smashed into that very spot not five meters away. Several Marines fell, including one a few meters further than me from the impact. I was untouched. I had had this kind of luck before, moving as almost instantly a mortar round lands on the exact spot I had just left, killing or maiming those around it. Staying alive was partly luck, I guessed. But I also thought it might be preordained one way or the other. You never knew, but I didn't want nor did I think it would happen to me. I suppose there were others who thought the same who had already bought the farm.

The Numbers Game

ONE OF THE FIRST pieces of data always wanted in the field after battle was the count of dead and wounded on both sides. A game was being played with the numbers. We would give the enemy figure in two ways—the actual number killed and the probable. Some units, I had heard, never counted actuals unless the bodies were actually stacked up and counted. Our unit, and I suspect most of the other units, would poll the troops to determine the number of the enemy killed. It became a far more fictional than real method of accounting.

I felt we had been hammered by the NVA a number of times due to our stupidity and our noisy helicopters. How could you ever really hide your position? It was a decision to use mobility and power; it was a choice to out-muscle the enemy, not out-smart him. *Time* magazine continued their story of our battle: "It turned out to be the last North Vietnamese thrust near Khe Sanh. When the Marines stormed up 881 North, twelve days after the battle for the valley had been joined, the communists had withdrawn into Laos. The Marines counted 575 enemy bodies on the three hills and estimated that air and artillery had taken at least another 600 communist lives—a 'tremendous toll,' said General William Westmoreland, who visited the battlefield. 'I don't think the battle is necessarily over,' he added. 'I anticipate further fighting in the area.'"

It did not surprise me that the *Time* article started with a deprecation of the NVA exaggerated figures: "Forced to rationalize defeat after defeat in South Vietnam, the Viet Cong and the North Vietnamese army have been desperately searching for a major military or psychological victory. They have lately been emboldened in the search by highly exaggerated reports from their commanders in the South, who often multiply the number of U.S. dead by ten or fifteen in order to please their bosses up North."

I picked up an ammunition pouch and a Chinese-made hand grenade from a dead NVA non-commissioned officer that my men had just killed in our move through the saddle. I would have liked a Russian AK-47 as a souvenir, too, but we had been told that the Navy squids back on the ship just stole all that stuff when it came in. I began to realize that I did not want to be a heroic charge-the-hill Marine, but I still wanted the trinkets of war to show to my friends back home.

Ambush

OUR COMPANY STAYED ON a hill next to 881 North. This was also the battalion CP. We went on long patrols further to the north, combing the area for remnants of the NVA army we knew were there. Spotter planes had seen them moving supplies by elephants through the jungle. I was impressed with the way they camped, the way they moved. On one patrol I suddenly realized we were in a heavily bunkered area. There were enough bunkers for a whole regiment, all cleverly disguised, even from the ground. They lined a ridge midway up, since our B-52s had a preference for hitting either the draws (the ridges toward the bottom of the hill) or the tops of ridgelines. They had cut a tree here and there, not noticeably disrupting the landscape at all. There were even tunnels between what appeared to be the command bunkers. They moved on foot, carried rice, and lived on less. We were more brutal, more evident in our movement and campsites. We were ugly Americans.

After several days of patrols we were back at our hill, which in only a few days felt like a permanent base. The foxhole I shared with one of my platoon's two corpsmen and my radio operator was a comfortable four feet deep, relatively safe from mortars except from a direct hit. Foxtrot Company was out on a long patrol. We heard fire in the distance—a lot of machine guns and small arms. Word came quickly over the radio that Foxtrot Company had been ambushed in a clearing. Nearly everyone was hit. They were pinned down, snipers having a field day. It happened fast. Twenty or thirty able survivors were returning fire but the area was not secure enough for medevacs. As had happened so often, the NVA would stop their fire, knowing the choppers would come in. Then they would open up as the helicopter rested vulnerably on the deck. It had already happened here. One of the two pilots was shot through the neck with a .50-caliber round. He died instantly. The other pilot got the CH-46 chopper out of there.

Ray, my company commander, sent me over to see Pappy. He was going to helilift my platoon in on a hill about a thousand meters from Foxtrot Company. I would move down the hill and secure the landing zone so they could bring in the medevacs and get the dead and wounded out. In less than ten minutes, a two-hundred-man company had been reduced to less than fifty Marines who could fight.

We moved down a steep trail. I could tell we were being watched the entire way. There were whistles that I knew were not birds, as though our exact number was being counted off and transmitted to a waiting encamped ambush. We stumbled on a large gravesite with shallowly buried fresh NVA corpses. The brass wanted the number dead—more of the numbers game. We were risking exposure and wasting time for the sake of statistics. It would have taken too long to comb the area and count all the graves. I guessed and reported a count. I felt safer moving. Besides, there were Marines bleeding to death below us. As we moved into the cleared area, I placed two squads at opposite ends behind the tree line. There was intermittent firing. We circled the area. The remaining NVA retreated. We called in the choppers. I knew it was all being watched.

Foxtrot had made the classic error. They walked into an open area in column rather than moving on both sides in the tree line. A few snipers had sucked them into an assault. Then they were wiped out from the side by well-dug-in machine gun nests. The new company commander, a fresh captain, had not been in the woods for some time; it took a while to develop that sixth sense, but he had lost his company, and now all four companies in the battalion had been hard hit. The battalion was at less than half strength. They were running low on body bags back at the Khe Sanh airbase.

I marched back up the same path with the two squads of my platoon that had gone to the aid of battered Foxtrot. One squad had remained behind to cover our flank from the high ground. When I got back, I found Pappy there with my squad. He had brought in a 106-mm recoilless rifle and a few more Marines to help cover us from the knoll. It was definitely not standard practice for the battalion CO to be way the hell out front with just a squad. They had fired the giant 106 at a couple of NVA who shot at them from nearby. Pappy had even gotten a few shots off with a borrowed M-16. He spent the night with my platoon on this high ground. Before he had sent my platoon out on this mission he had told me, with affection, to watch my ass. He didn't want to lose another Princeton man.

Out of the Hills

A DAY LATER, BACK at our more familiar camp near 881 North, we learned a fresh battalion would be coming to replace us in these hills. We would fly from Khe Sanh to Da Nang and then back to the ship. We would get to Subic Bay and liberty in the Philippines or perhaps Taipei. We would get a new supply of officers and troops. I had one of the strongest platoons in the battalion. I had lost about a third of my men. It was a quiet May afternoon, sunny and green. I had seen green for so long, green and brown. Our jungle utilities would become almost the color of the earth around us. They would get stiff and rot off after a few months. Once in a while we would get a new issue. It was like a layer of skin; you never took them off.

I peered out over the mountains. I supposed it must be beautiful, looking at the ranges that extended into Laos not far away. But I was sick of green, green trees, bushes. It was only beautiful if there was some contrast. I dreamed of cheeseburgers and ice cold Cokes and streets and cars and different colored clothes. I had seen a *Time* magazine that talked about "a happening" in San Francisco. Allen Ginsberg had paraded with thousands of multi-colored outfitted hippies through the streets. They smoked grass and sang songs. It seemed like fun. There was no reason for the event. It just was. I liked that idea.

Khe Sanh, when we returned, was busier. It had the same red clay. There were new craters. It had been shelled from the hills with 120-mm mortars. Two of my close friends from basic training were part of the relief battalion. We talked about our experiences over a few welcome beers. We had only an hour together. We had all been so gung-ho only months before. We had talked of being career Marines. But now we had been under fire and seen stupidity and death. We wanted to stay alive, to keep our Marines alive. We couldn't care less about killing NVA. We couldn't care less about communism or capitalism. It was all a crock. We just wanted to get home and live normal lives with our friends. Our wants had become simple: the ecstasy of not being shot at, not having to watch endlessly for death's weaponry, and being able to sleep an entire night through. We agreed on it all. We said good luck. We looked into each other's eyes with a new knowledge of life. It was precious.

Still, we mocked the large air force bunker at Khe Sanh. It had a sign forbidding any but their own personnel. What a bunch of chickens, we laughed. Were they scared of us? Deep down, the romance was alive. We were proud to be hardened, knowledgeable veterans of combat. We were better than civilians. We had tasted war.

The Tripoli

THERE WERE DIFFERENT SHIPS waiting for us offshore, brand new amphibious assault ships, designed especially for Marines and helicopters. My new home was the USS Tripoli. It was smaller than the Princeton, but it was new and neat, air-conditioned, and cool. There were big meals and cheeseburgers at night. There was time to read and to check the unreliable M-16s.

A congressional investigation had been started regarding the M-16s. Pappy had stood behind his men. He insisted we were right—it was not our failure to keep the weapons clean. There was something wrong with the weapon. The big brass flew in on choppers. Several squads had lined the stern of the ship. Our weapons had been cleaned three times, inspected and re-inspected; the conditions were ideal. We fired into the sea and rifle after rifle jammed.

We were right. We wanted the reliable M-14 back, but that was not going to happen. We were told to use the M-16 only on the semi-automatic position. The "matty Mattel" toys—our nicknames for these new weapons, which seemed like someone's idea of a bad joke—also had a tendency to fall apart. Some of my men were using chewing gum to keep several of the pins from falling off the weapon, making it useless. Still, the position from up high was not clear even after the experiment. I felt apathetic. They were all fools at a fool's game. You could afford to be a fool when you weren't part of the cannon fodder, when you were just one of the strategists moving pins on a map and counting hills won and lives snuffed.

Going Back In

THE PROMISED TRIP WAS not going to occur. The Philippines were out. Taipei was out. We were going in again. We had fresh troops. We had a ceremony for the dead on the deck of the ship. There was a tentative plan to lead us in North Vietnam twenty miles into the enemy's own country—a major escalation. It was a high risk Inchon strategy, to pull the enemy up from the south. We would be dropped inland and fight our way to the sea.

Locker Box Jones wasn't going on this operation, he announced. He had seen enough death, I thought. How many times had the company turned over through dead and wounded since he had been there? Battalion commanders were only put into the field for six months; the strain was so great. They had to maintain morale. They had to be up, enthusiastic, tough—even after the hammering we had had at Khe Sanh. There was only so much death and suffering that a human could take. The First Sergeant had reached his limit. I was beginning to wonder about myself.

Sgt. Mack, my platoon sergeant, was getting short. It was nearly his last month of the thirteen in Vietnam. The first month and the last month were regarded as the most dangerous. Not many got to the thirteenth month in the infantry, but it was considered difficult because the tendency was to reflect too much on getting out and to not pay enough attention to the situation at hand. Such reflection often meant less wariness—a few less decibels of caution that could

Sgt. Mack talking up the South Vietnamese soldiers

cost it all. Sgt. Mack had seen enough a long time ago. He was a good sergeant—competent, respected by the men.

He had been the platoon leader for several months before I arrived, when there was a severe shortage of second lieutenants. He was transferred to platoon sergeant of the weapons platoon, which in Vietnam was normally divided among the three rifle platoons in each company. This meant traveling with the company CP which was several degrees safer than moving with a platoon.

Sgt. Mack was happy he would not be with the first platoon on this next operation. The plan had changed somewhat. The battalion would not go into North Vietnam but we would be dropped along the Ben Hai River in the center of the DMZ. It was a major escalation of the war, the first time a large unit other than small reconnaissance teams had been sent into the DMZ. There might be two divisions of NVA south of us while directly across the river was North Vietnam, their larger artillery positions, and ready sources of resupply. Our company was going in first. My platoon would be the first to hit the LZ and God knew what else. I didn't blame Sgt. Mack for being happy. I was happy for him, too.

It was the best of the Hollywood-esque extravaganzas thus far. Eight-inch naval guns pounded the impact area and suspected artillery and rocket positions in North Vietnam. The Phantom jets were blasting away at possible artillery pockets as well. We jogged in neat files onto the waiting CH-46 choppers. The ships disappeared beneath us. We were going very high. The Navy was pumping in the fire, and even they were receiving stray fire from the shore. We were flying at 10,000 feet, above the high trajectory of the Navy guns. They would lift their fire just as we started a deep dive into the DMZ. You could see the explosions on the ground as we descended quickly. Another lieutenant told me later he could see the Russian-made SAM missiles shoot up like telephone poles at our close air support just to the north. The plan was that we would patrol around the river for a few days hoping to draw up the NVA units to the south. Then we would head south as another regiment moved north from Con Tien. It was a squeeze play. This was no guerrilla operation. This was a real, mean, conventional war. We were jumping in their backyard.

I always thought it was safer not to mark the LZ with preparatory fire. It just let the enemy know where you were going. Sure enough, when we landed there were several mortar rounds landing there, too. You could tell the NVA forward observers were just zeroing in because only single rounds fell. Once they had a fix on the location, then the barrage would start. Rather than secure the LZ as was the practice, I just ran my platoon another several hundred meters and radioed that the LZ was hot. There was a lot of confusion initially. The whole battalion was coming in several waves. I don't think we landed where planned, but you were always ready to be a few thousand meters off when you came in with choppers. Our small spotter planes were being shot at from the south with .50-caliber guns. You could see the tracer rounds in the sky. I knew this would be no easy walk through the woods.

The Dilemma

THE BATTALION CP WAS on a plateau that looked across the river into North Vietnam. Pappy was using the recon platoon as a guard for the battalion command unit. He had all the other companies deployed. Pappy didn't like to use recon much. The recon platoon was angry to have been given such insignificant duty. The recon platoon commander carried a deck of cards, all the ace of spades. It was a symbol of death. They would leave them on the bodies of the enemy dead, he told me. I would have been happy to trade places with him instead of poking around in the bush looking for trouble. I didn't think he'd been really kicked around by the NVA yet. Once you'd really been in the thick of it, you never looked for trouble. You knew it wasn't fun.

Our company was to move through an abandoned village at the edge of the river. The third platoon was in the lead. They moved down an old trail and received fire as they moved into the clearing about fifty meters from the village. There was a team of cameramen from CBS shooting moving pictures of our operation. They traveled with the company CP. They were Japanese. Ray, the company commander, told me my platoon was going in next. The third platoon had pulled back. They had taken one KIA. The body was still on the trail. It was a Marine practice to always get out our dead. It was part of the Marine code. I didn't think it made sense when it meant risking more lives. But it was a matter of pride. That's what made us different.

I told the CO that there was no way I was going down the same path with my platoon just to walk into an identical trap. I wanted to envelop from the east. Ray said there wasn't time. There's never a clear choice in combat. I was going in with my platoon.

I remember the look on Starr's face. He was my radio operator then. Starr was lying on his back propped against a rock with all his gear strapped on, including the radio. He looked tired and lethargic. I told him we were moving out. Starr didn't move. His face was clammy and moist. His eyes had that distant, half-asleep look in them. I had to tell him several times to get on his feet. I moved just behind the first squad as we angled slowly down the trail toward the village. The company CO was in a foxhole on a small ridge just above the village. The CBS cameramen decided to stay with him.

I left the rear squad on the side of the hill. They could partially cover us after we got on line and moved through the village. When the first squad had reached the dead Marine from the third platoon, the machine gun nests opened up on us. Three men were hit right away. A round ripped between my legs and blew dirt on the hill's edge a few feet from me. We hit the ground. I heard screams for corpsman. My first squad leader was on the radio just twenty-five yards ahead. Starr was dead, hit in the head. I got Cpl. Smith, my best machine gunner, to get his M-60 lined up to return fire. It was hard to tell exactly where the enemy fire was coming from. There were well-dug-in bunkers as close as twenty or thirty meters across the open space. They had us pinned to the earth with nothing in between to protect us from the steady spurts of machine gun fire. Then Smith was hit. He was bleeding to death, hunched over his machine gun. The corpsman at the rear of the platoon had run down, hearing the wounded cries. I told him not to go up the trail. He ran anyway. His name was Ellis. He was shot dead seconds later.

I had a forward observer with me and his radio had a direct linkage to the artillery base at Con Tien to our rear. Con Tien had been overrun a few months earlier, and now we were at the far edge of their range to the north. We were so close to the NVA that any support by artillery was like calling it in on your own head. But I saw no other answer. My Marines were getting knocked off one by one. We called in smoke rounds, which are not as deadly as the usual explosive shells. We would probably take casualties with our own artillery, but it was better than the slow suicide of waiting for the bullets to find you. At least it might give us cover to pull back. We were lucky—the smoke rounds came in on target. The shrapnel flew over our bodies that clung desperately to the earth. We pulled back, up the trail. My rear squad had been firing away and another squad from the third platoon had been brought up to try and cover us as we scrambled back up the hill.

I had lost most of the first squad. Two men came in later, having been cut off in the ambush. They had fought hand to hand with several NVA. One had been literally jumped on from behind. His rifle had jammed. He took off his helmet and beat the NVA soldier to the earth, then shot him with his own pistol. Five of my Marines were still down the path. They were dead. We had gotten the wounded out.

I learned much later that my mother and grandmother saw much of the battle on CBS news. They saw my company CO describe his first platoon pinned down by enemy fire. They heard him describe that the first platoon commander was calling artillery in on his own position. They heard the crack of small arms only a few hundred meters away. They heard the roar of artillery shells on their final descent and they heard the impact. They saw the concern on my CO's face. They saw the sweat streaming down the faces of the Marines who even at this distance from the battle had to stay low to avoid the spray of rifle and machine gun fire. They knew who my CO was. They knew where I was. It was all on TV. It was the 6 o'clock news.

That night Pappy called me over. He put his arm around me and said, "You got hit hard, didn't you, son?" He asked me how many of my Marines were still on the battlefield and how we ought to go in to get them out. We should envelop to the east, I replied. Pappy looked tired. I could have cried as I talked of my dead Marines. Pappy had already called in the air. They were dropping napalm on the NVA bunkers. Tomorrow we would go in again, this time with two companies. Foxtrot would envelop from the east and I would take the same path down to claim my dead and search the bombed village.

Foxtrot Company was angry. They thought we ought to do our own work and claim our own dead. I didn't blame them. Corporal Smith was still hunched over his machine gun. Ellis was nearly kneeling still, fallen over another dead Marine he was trying to save. Rigor mortis had set in. They were stiff and immobile. They had begun to stench and to turn that deep shade of brown that came with death and baking in the Vietnam heat. Corporal Smith just looked asleep. He was black to begin with. He would have done anything I asked of him. He was one of my best. I hated this war. I felt rage in my chest.

Pappy Leaves

THE NEXT DAY PAPPY left. His back had been bothering him for months. The battalion doctors told me he shouldn't be in the field at all; they had been giving him drugs. Perhaps Pappy had seen enough. Vietnam was like running marathon after marathon. It didn't take long to wear down your body. It was your mind that seemed to get eaten away, slowly—through numbness, the countless number of dead, cold apathy, and a sickening depression.

I still had anger and fear. I felt sick when Pappy left. I felt alone. He had lasted longer than any battalion commander I knew. He had led two battalions and seen hundreds of his Marines die. He had been fighting the bloodiest part of the war along the DMZ, yet I had seen no one able to take it without finally succumbing. There was no one who could maintain enthusiasm for war when you were in the thick of it. There was no romance in the end, just more flailing away 'til you cried uncle or the bullets caught you.

The battalion executive officer took over. He was a big, heavy, slow-talking major. We stayed on the same plateau for three days and ran patrols off it. It did not seem wise to stay in one spot so long.

I felt nervous. Why weren't we moving south as planned? When Pappy was around, at least we knew what was happening. He was always clear about his strategy. Pappy knew the game of war. He knew when and how to move. I was worried now—I did not have the same confidence in the major.

Hammered

WE WERE MOVING BACK into the battalion CP from a day-long company patrol. Another company was already in the area covering the perimeter. My platoon was in the middle about a hundred meters from the northern rim of the perimeter line. It was overcast, cloudy. Suddenly, an artillery round hit nearby, then another, then a dozen, and then it was havoc. We had been caught in the open. We had stayed in one spot too long. They hit us with howitzers, and mortars, and 140-mm rockets. The rockets screeched as they flew over your head. There were explosions all around, men crying for the corpsman. We just hit the deck. Running would have been insane. It would mean being cut to ribbons by the exploding shells all around. Some of my men wanted to run back down the hill away from the center of this pounding fusillade. I screamed at them to stay down. I wanted to run myself but I knew that meant certain death.

It was the most fearful moment I had ever experienced—thinking that in any second a rocket would land right on top of me and blow me into pieces of smoking flesh and blood. It was ugly. I had an overpowering feeling of total annihilation—a feeling of nothingness, of complete emptiness. I was angry at myself for having gotten into this incredible situation. I didn't have to come to this war. I didn't have to be blown away on this hill for no reason at all. And ideologies had no meaning in war. There was no reason to fight and die for anything. I just wanted to live. I prayed to God to give me another chance. Don't let me die. I knew I hadn't finished. There were still things to live for.

A 105-mm howitzer hit six feet from me. I could hear it come in. I thought it was the end. It blew a hole a foot deep and three feet wide. Shrapnel cut through my pack. The shock knocked me out. Coming to in a daze, I could not hear. The ground shook with the jolts of more incoming rounds. I felt so incredibly trapped. I felt my being about to be forcibly disintegrated. Death had no meaning. It felt like the end of it all. It was the smell of rotting bodies and vomit, and aching thirst. It was a nauseous, total dismemberment of it all.

We took over two hundred rounds. It cut my platoon to shreds. At least they had foxholes in the battalion area. We were just on the edge, lying in the grass. They had not been able to call in air support because of the temporary cloud cover. The NVA waited for just the right moment. The air and artillery were responding back now but the damage had been done. We had stayed too long on this hill and had been hit hard. Some of my men were just crying. They had lost it. Too many of their friends had been hit. I moved those that were left into some trees. I put them in ranks in platoon formation. I don't remember what I said. I just knew they needed some sort of structure. The formation, bizarre as it was next to North Vietnam soil, was a return to the discipline that was the basis for being a Marine. I had to get some sense of order back in their heads. They had become almost catatonic. And most of them were cut and bleeding. Some were dead. I forget details. We moved back into the battalion area. The medevacs were starting to come in. I passed a foxhole. Sergeant Mack was lying back in it, his eyes closed. He had taken a direct hit in his hole. He was dead.

There was a deadly quiet before the choppers came in. A small South Vietnamese unit was with the battalion CP as well as quite a number of correspondents and photographers. When the medevacs came in, both the Vietnamese and the correspondents raced on board while the wounded lay outside. We had to pull them out, practically at gunpoint. A few more shells hit the area. They were panicking. It was a rude kind of cowardice, to escape when others might die for need of medical help. I understood it, though. I would have liked to fly away, too.

The March South

AT LAST WE WERE marching south. That probably meant more fighting, but movement also meant a moving target, not the sitting ducks we had allowed ourselves to be. With Pappy gone, I did not feel confidence in the battalion's ability to respond. I wanted out of there. I had six men left in my platoon although I had landed a week earlier with a reinforced rifle platoon of nearly sixty. It was no longer a platoon; we were just survivors.

I traveled with Ray, my company CO, since I had no real platoon anymore. A number of them would return since none had actually been killed in that incredible artillery barrage, but nearly all of them were full of shrapnel to varying degrees. It was my platoon that was hit hardest. We were close enough to the battalion CP that we caught all the incoming fire, and we were too far from the battalion perimeter to find any protection in the foxholes there.

We were headed south. It was hot—the NVA were shooting .50-caliber machine guns at our spotter planes. We took a couple of mortar rounds nearby. No one was hit. It was hot, very hot, the way it can get sometimes. We were out of water again, like so many times before, and knowing that we would not be resupplied 'til dusk bred that kind of ugly parched feeling that extended from your tongue and throat all the way down your intestines. It made me dream of Coke pouring over a glass filled with ice, that lovely crackling sound. You knew if you didn't get water you'd be dead, but dreaming of that sweet sound seemed to help quench your thirst.

You'd risk getting shot at if they would just bring water. We called for water—"Sorry, later in the day, maybe," they said. The choppers were committed on some operation. I knew it was untrue. It was lunchtime on the ship. The bastards were drinking lemonade and eating on white tablecloths in the officers' mess. They had beer stashed in their rooms from pit stops they'd make in Da Nang, and hot showers at the end of the day. Sure, they bought the farm with regularity, too, but they didn't have to stay in that jungle and freeze at night and sweat all day. They could sleep a whole night, and rest long enough to face it another day. We were not able to stop. We had to move day after day. We heard the endless sound of incoming, the distant pop of the mortar round as it left the tube. You knew the mortar was seconds away then, high up in the sky forming a neat parabola on its trajectory. I was angry again.

The company CO was down with heat exhaustion, along with others that had reached their limits from lack of water. The medevac was called in. The march had also been temporarily stopped so they could bring water to keep the rest of us going. Ray turned the company over to me because the only other officer, Tom with the third platoon, was up ahead much further. I was glad Tom was still with me in the company. I trusted him. He'd been through the same battles and knew what to do. I looked at the gunnery sergeant and told him to get the men moving.

It was a relatively peaceful march to Con Tien. We crossed the beginnings of the McNamara Line, a 100-meter swath of dirt that was eventually to extend west to Khe Sanh. The Navy Seabees, the Navy construction battalion, had been hard at work clearing the jungle—probably their most dangerous mission in Vietnam. They had tasted mortar fire and the ever-present possibility of being overrun this far north.

We were supposed to meet the 26th regiment, which was marching north. Like a hammer and anvil we would catch the NVA in the middle. But the 26th just never got it together, and the hammer did not close. They were fairly new to Vietnam, having been just brought in country a few months earlier. Now they were lost; we heard the regimental commander had been relieved with his whole regiment floundering a few thousand meters too far south, not even to the line of departure yet. The NVA had slipped through, which happened easily enough in the thicket of foliage and trees and elephant grass. We could have walked past each other a hundred meters away and never known the difference.

So much the better; I did not want this fight. We had been told we would go back to the ships and at last get that promised trip to Subic Bay and liberty in the Philippines. My grandfather—an incredible person, I was told—had been killed there in a plane crash before I was born. He was General McArthur's aide along with Dwight Eisenhower. I wanted to visit there, to feel the soil. The earth had come to mean more to me, as though I could feel its history. I lived in it, lay on the earth each night, and had begun to feel more like an animal than I supposed. The dirt filled your pores, but there was no greasy feeling after a few days, no worry about getting dirty. You were the dirt. The line between you and the earth disappeared. You were part of each other. It felt very natural, very simple. Sometimes I wondered if life was meant to be this way.

In the Rear

WE WERE MET BY trucks at Con Tien which took us to Cam Lo. The ships had left without us. We had been chopped opcon (temporarily transferred) to the Third Marine Division, which meant they could do with us as they liked. Fortunately, we would get a rest, occupying another battalion's position while they took a turn in the field.

We had a new battalion executive officer, a reservist, and a lawyer who had decided to come on active duty and do his part in Vietnam. He was an administrative whiz. He had the whole clerical staff working full time on a mission of writing awards for the battalion. The task of writing them for our company had been assigned to me, so I had left my platoon to go to the battalion CP in Dong Ha. It felt like New York City in comparison to the boondocks we had been traveling in.

I wrote a letter home to my mother, grandmother, and sister. It was dated June 6, 1967:

"My writing has been negligent recently but I have been burdened by a load of administrative work—including the reworking of my citations to please a new finicky battalion executive officer. Pappy has left also with a painful back and the Major has taken over. The result is an inefficient battalion with no morale.

"I am at Dong Ha, in the rear with the gear, also doing an investigation on a traffic accident of all ridiculous things. The company is at Cam Lo, but we will all be back aboard the Tripoli sometime around the tenth, only to go on another operation around the seventeenth, destination and duration unknown. Your idea of writing something for the *Saturday Evening Post* is interesting. I don't know whether they would go for an anonymous writer as I am not particularly desirous of a general court martial. I'm afraid my feelings right now do not quite jibe with the party line. Perhaps I will be lucky enough to get home in time to go to war in the Middle East. I am tired of pushing a platoon through the weeds."

I enjoyed a more civilized life in the rear. I actually had a cot to sleep on. There was an officers' and staff NCO's (Non-Commissioned Officers) club to go to on the base, and the Seabees, close by, had built themselves a real castle. They had beer and movies at night. I would stumble back into the battalion area half-bombed, barely able to remember the code word that would prevent someone from drilling me in the middle of the pitch black nights.

There was a different set of adjectives that went with each grade of award all the way up to the Congressional Medal of Honor. I was trying to get out quite a number for the troops, who usually went unacknowledged, especially in the heavier combat when so many were lost and there was so little time for glory-making. So many deserved it just for the suffering, and I knew the game. Others had gotten a medal for much less.

Back Again

I DID NOT WANT to go back on the ship. We had a new company commander and a new executive officer. I had all-new troops. I did not have the same affinity for them—there wasn't time for that to develop. I didn't know if I really wanted to develop affinity anymore. It had hurt a lot to lose so many that I'd grown very fond of. In some ways I resented the new arrivals, perhaps because they were replacing my dead Marines. There was a handful left that had been with me since I'd arrived. I had only enough loyalty left for them.

Ship life was all right, but it meant more combat later. I was studying a Marine law course and was reading until the day and time came to make preparations for another landing. I finished a book called *Peter Abelard*. It was romantic and took my mind away from what was coming next. I packed it along with all my gear in a duffle bag. Before each operation we would pack all our belongings as though we had already bought the farm. It made sense. It was easier if you got hit for others to not have this odious obligation. It was like carrying your own cross.

We were headed back south of Quang Tri. We were going into a valley that belonged to the NVA and Viet Cong. No unit had ever ventured into this valley without incredible resistance. It was dense with vegetation, mountainous, and difficult to move in except via trails. It was a guaranteed fight. We would move along the coastal region first, then cross a river that led into sure battle. The new company commander and executive officer had not seen combat. They were nice and easygoing, but I would rather have been in charge. There was a need for more discipline with many new untested Marines. I had made sergeants out of men who should have still been PFCs. The men were good Marines, but they had not had the training expected at this level. They did not know enough to be good fire team leaders, much less good squad leaders.

I felt very distant as we started this operation. I felt as though

I hardly belonged to my own platoon. The battalion had turned over nearly twice since I had been there. I should have been dead or wounded in some hospital by now since most second lieutenants didn't make it past the first four months. I was overdue, going around for the second time. I felt more than seasoned. I felt ripe. I felt vulnerable.

As we moved into one village, the familiar crack of small arms fire erupted all around me. My lead squad was hit. Several rice paddy dikes separated us from the tree line where the fire was coming from. I had men dying that I could not help. I had them put out the bright gold flags from inside their helmets to make an arrow pointing to the enemy only fifty meters away. The arrow was to guide in close air support. Unfortunately, all the air support for the Navy, Air Force, and Marines was now under one command. You didn't know which of the three was coming to help. I trusted the Marine pilots. They had been trained to drop their arsenal in front of troops with accuracy. I did not trust the rest. We were asking for thousand-pound bombs which made damn big holes.

An Air Force covey (two attack aircraft) came in overhead. I talked them in on radio, but the bombs landed about a hundred meters behind us, away from the target. I was just thankful they missed by so much. It wouldn't have been the first time a Marine unit was wiped out by its own air support. I just thanked them for the good work. I didn't want them to take a second crack just because they felt they should accomplish their mission; not at my expense anyway. We finally got another company up on the flank and they swept through the village. I had more dead. I don't remember as much about this operation. It seems more like an early morning dream that fades when you wake. Part of me was not there anymore.

I remember another firefight in another village. I remember calling in a Huey gunship. The pilot landed near me, the only way he could contact me. He told me he had them cornered—there were more than a dozen in a hooch up ahead. I remember the fatigue of my Marines, and that we had not had water all day. We were getting mortared as we moved forward, and some men were bleeding to death with no water to even solace them in their pain. I remember saying "screw it" to myself. I was not taking them in an assault. We were the point platoon. I told the CO that we were pinned down and couldn't advance. After all, they had been moving us in so fast in order to get through the villages and reach some small hill that only had its elevation number as a goal, as if it were some god to be worshipped.

We would move in long dangerous columns, racing through the heat because some idiotic colonel on a ship looking at some frigging map had determined that this little knoll, with elevation such-and-such, was our next objective. The reality was that we were running into the open like ducks in a shooting gallery. It was the ultimate absurdity—chasing hills like some kind of Olympic cross-country event while the Viet Cong waited in the comfort of the shade for us to stumble into their line of fire. We were being used as decoys in the most blatant way. At least Pappy knew how to fight. I hated being cannon fodder for the pleasure of those who sat on a ship and had even more than just the luxury of drinking water and not getting shot at. The next day, as we moved through the sandy dunes between villages and vast empty spaces, I began to feel death all around me. I had not even learned the names of many of my new Marines—they were ghosts. I felt isolated and apart. I was moving faster and faster away, into a dreamlike fog.

The Crater

THE NEXT MORNING WE were to go across the river into the dreaded valley. We would commandeer villagers and bribe them to take us across in small boats. How crazy I thought. What a great way to get ambushed. We would spend hours crossing a river, giving any enemy a chance to mass and pick off the divided pieces.

I had an uneasy feeling that death was waiting across that river. I didn't know for sure. You never knew for sure, but I could see the ambush. I could feel the small arms fire that would rake our flesh into eternity.

That evening, as we moved onto a sand ridge that would be our home for the night, we took mortars and small arms fire. As rounds landed nearby and the shrapnel was flying on both sides of me, I dove into a crater left by a B-52 bomber. My bad knee gave way and contorted under me. The familiar swelling and stiffness began to appear. It was bent but would not bend. I could barely limp with my one good leg. I was medevaced back to the ship. The battalion doctor told me that the ligaments and cartilage had been torn again, and that the knee was already arthritic. I was to leave through Da Nang. A helicopter would take me to an Air Force hospital. From there I would fly to Japan and the Navy hospital in Yokosuka.

My platoon was ambushed just on the other side of the river. Several were killed, many wounded. One lost an arm, another lost a leg. I had seen that movie before. It was a bad movie. I was conscience-stricken because I had not faced death with my Marines.

Yokosuka

PAPPY HAD A RULE for everyone in the battalion. If he asked you how you were, your reply was always, "Excellent to outstanding, sir." It helped morale. It established a criterion of optimism, whatever the conditions. Lying in bed in the hospital in Yokosuka was the first time I had really felt excellent to outstanding since I had left California. In fact, I couldn't remember when I had ever felt better. I was in a neat, clean, bare hospital room by myself, listening to the peaceful sound of the air conditioning coming through the vents. It was beautiful in its simplicity. I just lay there in near-ecstasy enjoying the peace—enjoying just being alive and resting with the comforting drone of cool air. It was a transcendent experience to be so content, so blissfully happy in that silence. Being alive was enough, the most incredible joy. I told myself I would never need more than this, than to just sit and listen to the quiet noises of life.

It seemed like I was getting a lot of attention. Several different nurses had come to see me the first day. I learned after that they were just checking out the new Marine officer. It was a forgotten pleasure to see American women. I was amazed at how much I enjoyed seeing children playing in the grass. It seemed incredible to me that people could really fight and kill each other. If children could only be on each battlefield and frolic in front of the armies, the contrast of simple joy juxtaposed on ugly massacre should be enough to stop the fighting. The generals should take their kids to war, I thought; then there could be no war. War was a product of separating various facets of life. To exist, war had to be made independent of and distant from family life. War could not coexist with the simple joys of fresh air and children playing. I was happy to be away from the sounds of war. I was so very happy to be alive.

I weighed 147 pounds when I arrived, my waist having descended to twenty-six inches from a normal thirty-six. I was a stick. I ate three meals for every one, as though I was making up for lost time. I started to write about Vietnam. It was fiction in form, although I recalled incidents as I had observed them. I wrote all one afternoon while sitting in the sun at the officers' club pool. I got sunburned. I wrote nearly seven pages before I realized I would be in pain the next day. The writing began to bother me; it didn't feel right. I didn't want to think about war much less write about it.

I called home while I was in Japan. Randy, a roommate at Princeton and a Marine pilot, had been killed in a training accident over Georgia. His plane had gone down, the body not even recognizable. He was very religious. His last year in school he went to mass every morning, and at some level I thought he must have known, nearly a year before. He had been getting ready; he had been talking to God for some time. It seemed ironic that I was still alive after all the combat and that I should learn of Randy's death while still in Southeast Asia. It made me stop. It made me think again of the vulnerability of life. Somehow it was different when such a close friend left forever. I could imagine us drinking a beer and laughing or Randy reading excerpts from *Catch 22* back at Quantico. I had been deprived of our reunion.

I don't remember if I cried. I think I just sighed with that heavy sinking feeling in my chest, almost catatonic, as though there was only so much emotion in me and the bottom had already been reached. Like the unfinished novel that burned up in the sun, along with my body, I was just tired of it all. I didn't want to hear any more of death. In the hospital they called it "combat fatigue," a name that gave credibility to this special state of mind which was more of an emptiness of mind and feeling. War just took away your heart and mind and drained out whatever your soul was. It was like being some sort of abandoned ship, still puttering along on the open seas, but just a shell—afloat yes, but hardly alive. In reality, you're already a ghost, just waiting for the sea to swallow you into eternity. But there was also a certain stillness—a stillness that felt very, very real.

On the Way Back

A MONTH LATER I was able to get around just enough to be sent to Okinawa temporarily before being sent back to the States. I was on "The Rock," as we called it, for nearly a month. One of my friends from Princeton who had joined the Marines was also on Okinawa. Ernie had already been wounded twice. Shortly he would be going back to Vietnam. He enjoyed it. Ernie loved his platoon and wanted to get back. It was quite a reversal from his feelings in school—he had proclaimed at Princeton that fighting was not for him. Ernie was a gigantic man, soft-spoken, not needing to prove his manliness to anyone. Meanwhile I, in my gung-ho reverie, was itching to go get the VC. Now Ernie seemed to enjoy the sport of war. I was wondering if the fighting he had been in had been different from what I'd seen. I just couldn't imagine how anyone could want more suffering, but I gave him credit for being strong, stronger even than his looming, quiet physique. I learned a few months later that Ernie had returned and lost an eye in combat.

What surprised me more while I was on "The Rock" was learning that another friend from school—a year behind me, a rugby player, a strong man, and a close friend—had committed suicide. I couldn't understand suicide. I had tried so hard to stay alive. How could anyone take their own life? I was still feeling that preciousness of existence, of waking to the warm sun and having breakfast without fear of life-ending bullets. I was told he had become depressed and quiet. His thesis in religion was not going well for him. He burned it up one evening and then blew out his brains with a shotgun. If I had only known his feelings; if I could just have talked to him. If I could have just told him about war and about the beautiful sound of the air conditioning in my hospital room in Yokosuka. The irony of it burned me inside. I had been crazy, the one who had romanticized war to my friends. I had proclaimed to be one of the glorious professional soldiers, and yet it was those who had been more cautious, who had smiled at my bravado, and who no doubt were convinced I was a lunatic—they were the ones who were falling off like flies.

Back to D.C.

A MONTH LATER I was back in D.C. I saw my friend Pat, a platoon commander from Foxtrot Company who had been part of the massacre north of Khe Sanh. He was in a body cast that left only one arm free. He had been that way for months. One leg was going to be shorter by an inch, but he hoped to be allowed to stay in the Marines and additionally go to flight school to become a pilot. Pat had had enough of the grunts. The lifestyle of the air wing seemed more appropriate. He figured Vietnam would be long over by the time he was a pilot and combat-ready again. But I figured some idiotic politician would have us in another war by then and ruin his scheme.

I joined the service battalion at Marine Headquarters near the Pentagon. One day, I was at my mother's apartment in Georgetown when the doorbell chimed. As I opened the door, I greeted a face that was even more startled than my own. Al was a friend from our training as second lieutenants. He was one of the Ivy League warriors from Harvard. In an explosion he had lost some fingers and both legs, one above and one just below the knee. It had happened fairly early on his tour, and he was just about rehabilitated, meaning that they had taught him how to walk on his artificial limbs. He had come to see my mother and find out how I was faring in Vietnam. It seemed as though Al had accepted his fate and still faced life with great optimism. How different life had become in just a year's time.

The Job

AT THE BASE I was asked to work with the special committee on Vietnam matters for Lt. General Walt, the man who had managed all the Marines in Vietnam before and during the time I was there. We were doing research on the newspapers, determining their stand on various Vietnam issues. It was a top-secret job, but I don't remember ever reading anything top secret that I hadn't read earlier in a newspaper.

I watched different papers take certain consistent points of view on various aspects of the war. I watched the *Washington Post* move from a hawk to a milder, less supportive stance from the fall of 1967 'til the beginning of 1968. I read of a retired Army general who took a job with Colt's Manufacturing Company after Colt signed a big contract with the Defense Department for the manufacture of all the M-16 cartridges. There was speculation that Colt had used a faster firing round which was responsible for the jamming of the M-16 in Vietnam. I felt for the needless dead in my battalion who had assaulted bunkers and hills only to find themselves defenseless in their bravery. No one seemed to notice this issue. It died quietly in the back of the Congressional Record.

After several months, I felt I had learned the company line on the war completely. I had investigated from the French involvement in Indo-China through the SEATO agreement and our current buildup. I had read all the State Department propaganda and all the newspapers of note, pro and con. I knew the arguments inside and out. At the same time, I had realized in my research endeavor that there was no innate logic to foreign policy. It was whatever illusion those in power wanted to create and sustain.

I had also found out at the State Department, after much effort, that the SEATO Treaty—one of several reasons given for our involvement in Vietnam—had a very peculiar facet to its beginnings. The Southeast Asia nations were termed "protocol signatories." When I finally found out what that meant, I was shocked. It meant that South Vietnam, as well as Cambodia and Laos, did not actually sign the treaty. The only actual signatories were the U.S., Australia, France, New Zealand, Pakistan, Philippines, Thailand, and Britain; our presence in Vietnam was like some kind of Mafia protection racket. This apparently unasked-for protection was covered up with a term that cleverly disguised the lack of formal agreement between Vietnam and her so-called allies. I was even more amazed that none of the anti-war muckrakers had discovered this giant loophole in the party line.

The Protests

MEANWHILE, THE WAR BREWED on. I had missed, but not missed, the 1968 Tet offensive. I had made the beginnings of the shootout at Khe Sanh but was gone for the siege in 1968. I could read between the lines of the news reports, see beyond the lenses of the news cameras, and feel the suffering and see mayhem while order and victory were being projected back. I was glad not to be there and had greatly avoided thinking about it. The theater of the office had consumed my attention.

Two events caused me to think more seriously. The first involved a woman Marine who had principally been a lifeguard for the year or so she had been in the service. One day, she decided not to wear her uniform as a protest of the war. Her brother was in school and more actively opposed to the war, as most college campuses had become in the last couple of years. She seemed mostly unaware of the issues surrounding the war, more influenced by her brother and by the fun of upsetting an entire Marine Corps with so little effort. She had the press phoning constantly. At her small summary court martial, all the newspapers and half the TV stations were there—a great spectacle—everyone making a big issue about a uniform.

It was so completely absurd. It seemed to me to be a different kind of war, a war of words mostly. But it still encompassed similar elements to the romance of John Wayne that had entranced me at the inception of my military experience. I had wanted to prove myself as a Marine, and this war of words was just an arena for people to find their own heroic deeds, either for or against the war. That's what made it all absurd. Ideology was not relevant as I watched the spectacle of cameras and clambering reporters trying to get their questions in. The diatribe was not as brutal as being shot at, but it did not feel any more meaningful than the war itself, and the war had no meaning for me.

Later in the year was the candlelight march on the Pentagon, a hundred thousand or so marching to protest the awful war. My sister was a student at Vassar then. She was in the march. I was officer of the day at Headquarters Battalion. We were on alert. If things broke into violence at the Pentagon, the Guard Company would go in. I wore a .45-caliber pistol as officer of the day. It was the same weapon I carried in Vietnam, but in D.C. I had made practice of not putting any bullets in it. This evening was no exception, though I was glad to have the responsibility. I knew if our unit was somehow involved I wasn't going to let anybody fire anything, not with my sister in the crowd. I had no feelings about the war, for either side. It was just a bunch of people making a big scene. I enjoyed the theater aspect of it, but rightness or wrongness of either side was just not an issue for me then.

Checking Out

AS SPRING LOOMED CLOSER, so did the big change to a new phase of life. I had a chance to stay in the Marines—I had made friends who could influence the outcome. I was offered the option of staying in the Marines for two more years to write Marine Corps history in Hawaii. It was inviting in many respects. I had enjoyed my work on the special committee. I knew it meant time to myself, yet I also knew that if the war suddenly escalated, the historian might quickly be sent back across the "big pond." The infantry would be calling sooner or later anyway, and I had resolved not to return to the jungle.

I was beginning to really feel the change, as though I were being tossed out, projected from the big machine that had been my home. It was an uneasy feeling. The summer was planned out. I was to be a management trainee at a bank in Milwaukee. Part of me didn't want to work at all, but I knew the experience would be valuable, and I needed the money.

Two weeks before I got out of the Marines, I was promoted to Captain. A week before I got out, I went down to basic school in Quantico where I had started as an officer three years earlier. I sold all but one uniform to a new officer at the school. I also needed a haircut, but decided to let it go this last week. Selling the uniforms meant I was not going to participate in the active reserve. It meant leaving the Marines for good. I was looking forward to the summer—the quiet beauty of the lake in Wisconsin. I didn't shave the day after I got out of the Marines. I decided to grow a beard.

Getting the Inside Out
1972

FIVE YEARS AFTER RETURNING from Vietnam I started writing poetry. I didn't decide to. It just came out, out of nowhere, as if I was only the vehicle for some other entity that was doing the writing. Many of the poems were about being in combat, then being with myself, from the inside.

The Drum

Though he'd never killed
He dreamed of war
Perfect lines, green boats
raking sand. Metal mouths
hammering earth with
sledge driven echoes.
Hard men
Tight necks
Tired knees to
the quick beach. Pressing
Big bodies
through fragments of smoke
Bulldozers turned halfback

And always
The uphill heroes

Though he'd never killed
He came to war
Through forgotten rice fields
    Littered with tin cans
    Famine seeds from the victors
Through the thick smell of jungle
    Computer bombed
    Craters planted in rows
Through the dry rhythm of bamboo
    Clenched by a rotting hand
    The tight stillness of dead nerves

And from the elephant grass
The whispered touch of enemy cloth

Though he'd never killed
He faced a man
Brown eyes and khaki lips
Who breathed
    and had a brother
Who stared at leaves
    and had a sister
Who mixed the sweat
of his flat palm
    with dry granulated earth
Who wondered if the hunt's steel
    would rip the drum in his chest
Who waited in the quiet of half light
for the victor's stroke
    to seed earth with his
    empty veins
Who would cry for his mother
    one more time

Though he'd never killed
He came to war
As the drum beat earth
The earth fell still

Journal from the Other World

It came down
in the very final analysis
Compressed ... Compressed,
you're too
Compressed, just take life, let it
not the way you
would have guessed it
Now that I knew it all
Life and eternity
The icy stillness of tomorrow and
yesterday
but then
Compressed ... Compressed

Completely alone
No letting out or blowing up
Compressed ... Compressed,
you're too, let it, take life
Each day, not all eternity in a
moment
Just let, and then someday
You'll finally blow out your brains
To relieve the tension

This morning, the blowing up part
So final
Until
.. anytime I wanted
I could still, if I wanted
any time
Still, no promises
and as I said before

when it was over
I must be
Coming from the other world
as though one time, years ago
when the rockets were coming down
hard
and my men
Legs and arms
Hands and heads like so many
Pieces in the soup
The smell of dying even in the grass
and eyebrows
Compressed ... Compressed,
you're too
Let it, just not, easy

Because if you don't
Someday, the relation to the past
Searching for just the right struggle
The icy stillness of tomorrow and
yesterday ...
Compressed .... Compressed
or else
I know
in my chest
It would be too much.

PART II

Looking Back

2012

The Urge and the Emptiness

WHEN THE MARCH TO Baghdad started in 2001 and the news reported the Marines charging ahead, enveloping enemy positions, I could feel the urge to join—a fantasy urge, but that same, excited energy of a twenty-year-old to join the march, to engage the enemy, to be part of the action. I would daydream about being called back up, called back to take a platoon into the melee. I could hear the triumphal music and see myself moving out with the troops, surrounded by the dust and noise of Humvees, racing to the line of departure.

Somehow the urge, the pull, hasn't gone away after all these decades, even after having tasted the real thing—the acrid smell of war, the sickening stench of rotting bodies, and the wrenching despair when comrades died beside me. The urge surprises me. It surprises me that it's still in me, and I didn't even realize until the march revved up and the news showed the force moving forward that I would still be taken by the emotion, the emotion to go back to the fight.

But this emotion is countered by my memories of having tasted the real thing—memories that are hard-wired into my brain: the feeling of chilling emptiness, the nothingness that embraced me when the bombs were coming in and there was nothing to do, no place to run. There was nothing to do but wait, wait to get blown into nothingness.

The two conflicting emotions cross before me, like intersecting fields of fire—the urge to join the march is countered by my memories of combat and the nothingness now welded to someplace underneath my chest. I see the young men, soldiers and Marines, swept up in the urge—yearning for the point, to engage the enemy, to be part of the action. I know in time, in a short time, they will meet the other side, and then they will know, they will know both sides—the urge and the emptiness.

Forgotten Premonition

WHEN I LEFT THE Marines in 1969, my mother was moving and decided to unload the accumulated items that she had kept for me as I grew up, among that my baby handprint in clay, photos of our family in the early years, and a set of bound schoolwork from first through fifth grade. The school would take all our work for the year—penmanship, math, drawings, compositions—and bind it all together along with our grade reports in black and orange books, our school colors. I leafed through them, discovering a young boy I had forgotten. A sadness settled over me—a sadness for a past life when I lived mostly in the now, the next moment the only other thought on the horizon. There were no lingering memories, regrets or hauntings, inner deliberations of a future not yet emerged.

Then I read a fifth-grade composition with the title, *When I grow up I will be...* It reads: "When I grow up I will go into the Marine Corps. I will go to war. It won't be fun." This startled me.

Did I know then that I would go to war? Was it a forgone con-clusion? And how did I know that it would not be fun, as good a youthful description as could be? As a young boy I revered my uncle—a Marines' Marine, already a veteran of Iwo Jima and Korea, who had fought hand to hand in both. He had given me a Marine uniform, told me stories, and been a kindred spirit; he was more of a father to me than my real father was. Certainly he had influenced my decision to join the Marines.

But I had made the choice as a freshman in college to join the Marines, not as a ten-year-old fifth grader ... or had I? Had I made the decision back then? Was it pre-destination, and it was all planned out? Planned not by me, but by someone else, some outside force—out of time, out of my control? Has it all been planned and I'm just moving on the track? I don't remember writing this so long ago. I didn't write it. Someone else did.

The Dream

I DON'T REMEMBER WHEN this dream started—was it right after Vietnam or twenty years ago?—but it was a long time ago. The dream would play the same way, a dream I would always remem-ber when I woke up. And days later, years later, I would have the same dream. I am in a helicopter with other troops, and we are cir-cling the jungle, a large open area below surrounded by hills—big hills that are more like mountains. They, the dark-skinned ones, the NVA, are down below shooting at us. We are hit and start to lose altitude. We are going down. I hope we go down at the edge of the jungle, not in the open where there'll be no chance to escape into the jungle or to take to the hills, the only chance.

And we go down. It's near the jungle. We are being shot at. We race into the tree line and charge through the heavy brush and branches. The NVA are gaining, like those dreams where you can't seem to run fast enough, where your energy is not connected to your feet, and they are gaining. Then we come to this building, more like a castle, in the middle of this jungle. We race in and close the gates, but they beat their way in as we clamber up stairs to a big room near the top and bolt the doors. But the doors do not withstand the hoard that is chasing us. The wood splinters as they break in.

The room is full of butcher block tables. I am on one as the NVA come in with knives, ready for the slaughter. I have my K-bar knife out, ready to fight. But I know it will end. There are too many of them. I know it will end. As the first one comes at me—my K-bar raised, his knife raised, charging, just a foot away—I wake up. As if the film broke just at that frame, I wake up. But I know the end, even if the dream movie does not show it. But it never shows the end. It just comes back, every now and then, and plays the same scenes, exactly the same way. And it ends the same way, my K-bar raised, his knife raised, charging, just before the end.

The Officers' Reunion

IN 1996 WE HAD a reunion of the officers I had gone to Basic School with just after college. This was the first time we had gathered since graduating at the end of 1966 and being shipped off. We were raced through the once six-month course in four-and-a-half, given the ramp up for Vietnam and the thirst for young second lieutenants. Most of us had not seen each other since then, but most of us knew of each one who had been killed in Vietnam.

My friend Larry was a fellow platoon commander in my battalion. He had been shot during the same battle that Col. Ohanesian had died in. We both ended up stationed near each other after returning. I recall talking about our non-combat jobs, our frustrations with the bureaucratic life that was so different for us. Perhaps we talked about whether to stay in the Marines or what else to do—I can't remember. But I knew I was headed to another realm. I did not want to kill or be killed, not yet. I liked the peacefulness of just hanging out, the easy conversation, the escape from the office and the uniforms.

I hadn't seen Larry since then, some twenty-two years. He had stayed in the Marines. He was the battalion commander in Lebanon the day the Marine Barracks was assaulted and blown up. He was blown out of the building but survived. When Larry arrived for the reunion, his wife was pushing him in a wheelchair. He was able to get up and move on crutches a few feet to the table we were gathering at. He was the same Larry I knew before—easygoing, smiling, and yakking about our time together two decades ago as if nothing were different. As if not a thing in the world had changed.

Dateline Finds Us

THIRTY YEARS AFTER MY time in Vietnam, I got a call out of the blue from someone claiming to be from *Dateline NBC*. They were doing a show on a Marine who had been in my battalion in Vietnam and wanted to know more about a particular battle we were in. This turned out to be the battle Dave Hackett was killed in. They were also looking for a photo taken of the battalion while we were on Okinawa before going back in country, which I did have and sent to them. They asked me to send my reactions to the show after it aired.

We had such high turnover while I was there that I mostly remembered those that were there earlier on, before the churn of warm bodies kept coming in to replace the dead and wounded. This battle was the beginning of the run of casualties. I saw familiar faces though several decades had passed and the obliteration of our unit dispersed everyone, and they had disappeared from my life. The interactive relationship with NBC had become a central point that connected many of us again.

What surprised me was what had happened to my best and most together sergeant. Ransbottom had a successful career in the Marines and had come home, married, had kids, and had a good career. But twenty years after the war, he began hearing grenades, began feeling the battle return around him. Then he took a shotgun and blew his brains out.

I was stunned, saddened. I thought of his children, and how awful that must be for them. My chest ached, thinking how that might have struck my own daughter. I watch the newscasts of families at the military funerals of their sons and daughters, the rifle salute, and the folded flag being presented. Before the rifle salute and the flag, the Service acknowledges their bravery, who they were, and how much they meant. How their memory would live on. If I were their parents I wouldn't want to live. And even if I did want to live, I would feel dead inside.

My grandfather was in the Army and died in a plane crash in the Philippines before the breakout of WWII. He was an aide to Gen. McArthur along with his buddy Dwight Eisenhower. They were training the Philippine Army for a potential attack by the Japanese. Who says we were entirely surprised by Pearl Harbor? But that's another period of time that I don't fully understand. My grandmother used to say to me—I don't remember how many times, but many times—that when my grandfather died, "My life ceased to exist."

I wrote my reactions to the *Dateline* show and mailed it in. A half year later I got a call that they were going to repeat the show and wanted me to read the letter at the end. A TV crew arrived and spent hours arranging my office where I kept the photos of our company, my platoon, and one of Dave and me. They put in lights, reflectors, and even a track to move the camera as they filmed. It seemed overkill in such a small room—10 feet by 10 feet. Then I read the short letter over and over as they repeated the process from different angles and different heights—I must have read it twenty-five times. But it wasn't boring. It wasn't tedious. Each reading moved me closer, back in time to the battle—to a quiet, almost out-of-time quiet. As I watched the battle unfold again in my mind, I had no emotion, no feeling; I noticed each moment of action but without a sense of action, just the movement of bodies, jungle branches, smoke and recoil, explosions without sound.

This second *Dateline* version aired on July 4, 1997. Barbara

Walters started the program and said a young lieutenant who had been in the battle would comment at the end. I was at a family summer gathering that weekend. They were all watching. I stayed in the back. At the end when I began to read, the rush of emotion rolled in. My chest tightened as it always does. I tried to control the rush of sadness as I always did. But I could not, as I always could not. As my eyes moistened, I pulled into another room. I didn't want to show my family how much this moved me, how much emotion it evoked, how I could not control it.

The following year, a younger friend who had played soccer at Princeton asked me if I would come to the annual soccer team award banquet where a leadership award was given each year in Dave's name. Dave had been the Captain and was the most revered leader among the many who held that role. Would I come to talk about Dave? I didn't go. That year, I had contracted a rare disease, Guillain-Barré, which had paralyzed my legs. But I did go back to my office and put a talk about Dave on video. No lights, no camera track—I just put the video on a tripod, turned it on, and wheeled behind my desk to do it on my own. I read from my journal about my last moments with Dave—the story he told me about Big Lou, the way he stood amidst the firefight to pinpoint snipers, the shot that took him down, and his last moments beside me breathing, until he stopped. My chest tightened, but I held on. I knew this was for the team. I couldn't let go, let it out. I had to control; I had to clench the tightness so that the heaving wouldn't start. If the heaving started, it would be too late then.

Reunion for the Troops

THE FIRST REUNION FOR the troops took place three decades later in Stanley, North Carolina in 1997. I saw older men whom I remembered as being teenagers or just a bit older—it felt unreal. I didn't really know who had survived the war or life. Now, I saw only those that remained. Now, I was reliving the battles, walking the terrain, remembering the hills, remembering the ones who lost it on the hills. The battles were like scenes from a screenplay now, just without the bullets and mortars landing nearby. This first reunion put those scenes back on, taking them from the back of my mind to a slideshow in my head. It was like reviewing old movies, one scene at a time, remembering the cloud cover that day, or the recoilless rifle round that landed just a few feet away. I thought about how it could have been different, depending on where you were, at just that time, if you had been just a few feet one way or another.

It had been easier for most of us officers to move on, to leave the recurring scenes behind, and to walk out of the war theater into another life. Our lives looked a lot like the lives of people who didn't go to war, who didn't carry this theater with them that brought back scene after scene. We also had college and other chances that helped us move on. But this wasn't the case for lots of the troops that didn't finish high school in time before the war, that didn't have high school and college reunions to go to. This was their reunion. This battalion was their reunion, their first reunion. They didn't have any other reunion to go to.

Wayne's Story

WAYNE WAS AT THE battalion reunion in 1997 and had been in my platoon. He'd researched the Defense Department records and catalogued all the Agent Orange drops in the DMZ. He told me there were many more toxic chemicals than the well-known Orange. Wayne was 100% PTSD disabled. He had had cancer. He had also lost six of his children to various diseases. Wayne was convinced it was all because of Agent Orange. He showed me the data, all the places we had fought, and the timetables of the chemical drops and the locations which coincided.

Wayne was angry. He had a cause. Mostly he wanted the world to acknowledge the link and the pain and loss he has lived with.

Back when the airbursts of Agent Orange were planned, after the defoliation had done its job, not only were the forests destroyed but Wayne's cells were damaged, and then his sperm was damaged. This destruction passed on to his children, whose lives were blistered and cut off before they even saw light. Wayne was angry. I could feel it so strongly I felt like I had been the one who pulled the bomb bay doors that let the spray loose all over and around us. Had Agent Orange soaked into my pores in some way that changed who I might have been, who I am now, or how my emotions travelled with me? I hadn't thought about it before, but I did now. I don't know. I really just don't know.

It took the VA (U.S. Department of Veteran Affairs) decades to even acknowledge the potential causality, then even longer to offer help. As much as the politicians talk about looking after the heroes and publically praising the sacrifices of the veterans, how there could be an argument about what just might be? Proving causality is always hard, requiring tightly-controlled experiments conducted over decades—too long a wait to make much difference to the aging vets. Politicians praise the heroes when the public opportunity comes, but don't challenge the bureaucrats who carefully smother an admission that could translate into new expenditures. After all, they need to contain incremental costs.

My Radio Operator

BECAUSE OF THE *DATELINE* show, which became the clearinghouse to reconnect us, the 1997 battalion was born. Unlike today, where units were sent as a whole to Iraq or Afghanistan, we arrived individually from multiple locations to replace those who had fallen or who were lucky enough to complete their tour and go home. I'd been in touch with David, my radio operator and constant companion in Vietnam. He was a country boy from Tennessee with a slow drawl and a warm heart, a younger brother to me. I learned he was experiencing 100% PTSD. He had come home to the spits and jeers of his one-time hometown citizens, who were now mostly anti-war and more disappointedly, anti-veteran.

David had started drinking. He couldn't get away from the war. He had frightening flashbacks. He slept with his combat boots on, fearing a night attack, curled up in the fetal position, and waiting for the inevitable mortar rounds to come in. He had bouts of anger and threatened some around him that he would blow them away. He drank more and more and didn't work—couldn't work. He had emotional flare-ups all the time. The VA put him on drugs, heavy drugs, like Depakote and others. It put him in a daze. It kept him quiet—most of the time. When the *Dateline* interviewer asked him some pointed questions, David told him that if the show said anything negative about the Marine Corps he'd come to New York and shoot him dead. No one called him back to follow up. He thought that was amusing.

David's sister and her son, David's nephew, were taking care of him. He couldn't work. He couldn't drive. He had difficulty being with anyone else without getting angry. David paid many visits to the VA. Sometimes he would complain about the effects of the drugs. Sometimes he would threaten to kill the doctor treating him. They'd put him in psychiatric lockdown and given him even more drugs until he calmed down, and they sent him back to be with his sister, all quieted down now.

We would talk on the phone. He told me he used to play golf and was close to being a scratch player. But he couldn't do that now. David just stayed in the house and watched TV. He didn't want to come to the reunion, but I told him I'd get a room for both of us. I'd be with him the whole time and really wanted to see him. His nephew drove him the distance from Tennessee to the motel in Stanley. Like all of us, he was older. He moved slowly, talked slowly. He smoked frequently. Even that he seemed to do slowly— the haze of the smoke and the haze of the drugs mixing together.

I talked David into going to a nearby public golf course to play just nine holes. He could just ride if he didn't want to play. We rented clubs, got a cart. He did play with me. After a few shots, I could tell and David could tell that he still had the knack, the skill, latent from way back, several decades back. During our game, his energy broke through. He starting talking faster—talking like I remembered, like he remembered. He was cracking the golf ball, liking his shots, and liking himself. He had come out of the fog, way out of the fog. There was no fog now, just the young country boy I remembered when we were "in country." He was vibrant, alive. David was back.

Was it just that simple to awaken him? Why had they drugged him these many years when just a few holes of golf could bring him back to life? Now, I was angry. How could they? How could they not see, not try anything and just hammer him with drugs, stuff the poison down his throat so he would never be, never have a life? But I had brought him back through pure luck, not really trying—just wanting to do something with him that was from a time past, before the war, before the pain, before the drugs.

We drove back to the motel. David was high. He was good. He was back. He was up for meeting the others, going to the battalion lunch. But as we walked into the room, he began to slow down, to go back. I could see him lose the energy, lose the country boy. He pulled out a cigarette, and sat quietly in a chair. He didn't want to go to lunch now. I could tell. Just like that, David had gone back into the fog.

The M-16 Jam Revealed

AT THE BATTALION REUNION we recounted the problems of the M-16s jamming, the Marines found with a cleaning rod down the barrel, attempting in vain to clear the round and defend themselves from the on-rushing NVA soldiers. They were found just that way, frozen in death, bullets in their heads.

The reunion was made possible by the *Dateline NBC* show. The show was centered on one homeless former Marine from our company, but was also the link that allowed us to find each other after so many decades. The anger remained about the M-16s. They (up the chain of command) kept insisting it was because we did not keep them clean. But we had cleaned and cleaned and still they jammed. Sometimes the pins that kept it all together would just fall out.

Pappy had a whole platoon at the back of the carrier, with their weapons cleaned many times over, fire off into the empty ocean. A congressman was there to observe. Almost all of the M-16s began to jam. The problem was obvious, but it was more than just a problem. How could you send men to war with toys? They were like boys with spears against the raking fire that could only mean a final charge. We were sure this demonstration would send the true message home, that now Congress and the brass would quickly return our M-14s, and thus our ability to fight and survive.

Then, nothing. Then the same message came back that we had not kept our weapons clean. This was evil. This was wrong. They had called us liars, and said we were incompetent as Marines. This was an insult. This was a death sentence. We knew the true failings of the weapon had been covered up, but why, for whom, for what benefit? Was it a payoff by Colt? Or was it the stubbornness of those generals who made the purchase and did not want to admit a mistake, despite the dead then and the dead that would follow as an on-going memorial to their stain-free careers?

Fifteen years later, I got a call from a *New York Times* correspondent named Chris Chivers, who was writing a book on the evolution of the machine gun. He was writing a chapter on the M-16 and the problems encountered in Vietnam. His research had taken him to our company. He was collecting stories—the real combat where the M-16s had jammed, and our failed attempts to get the brass to understand. We wanted the M-14s back. You could leave them in the mud for a month and they would still fire.

Chris Chivers interviewed several Marines in my platoon. David, my radio operator, told him about the pins falling out, how these Mattel-like toy guns would just fall apart. He told him how he put chewing gum over the pins to keep them in, to make sure they wouldn't fall apart when he needed it to work. Another Marine, Roy, told him of his gun jamming as an NVA crawled out of his hole and took aim as he looked on defenselessly. Then Connie, the Marine nearest to him, fired at the last moment to save him, wondering as he pulled the trigger if his would fail and if he would be standing there as well to await the final bullet.

Chris's laborious, in-depth investigation had traced the cover-up—the refusal to accept, to admit that the M-16 was fallible, was jamming, and was just a prop in a war scene. Only the scene had turned real, the enemy AK-47s had real bullets, with death warrants for those that had only movie props—the M-16s were like plastic replicas, never meant to go to real war. The trail led all the way up to the commander of all troops in Vietnam, General Westmorland. He had made the choice to go with the lighter weapon for jungle warfare. That was not wrong, and not a bad choice. But to ignore the truth of the M-16 failures, to not admit to the reality of the dead warriors for the sake of maintaining the wisdom of his decision, his infallibility, his legacy—that was his choice, and a bad one. But this explains it all—the blanket of silence across all the Army and Marine combat units that suffered the same subterfuge. It did not go beyond him. He had suffocated the truth, as if he had held a pillow over each warrior, whose real weapon he had taken away, until they had no breath.

Guillain-Barré

ONE DAY, ABOUT THIRTY years after the war, my legs started to get numb. I thought it was a pinched nerve in my back. About thirty days after that first day, I couldn't stand up or walk. I crawled to the phone and called my doctor. They told me I had something I'd never heard of called Guillian-Barré syndrome, a kissing cousin of polio—paralysis that starts at your feet and moves up your body, inch by inch. The good news is that after about a year it goes away, in reverse, inch by inch so you can walk again and be normal.

It wasn't a big deal, just an experience for a time. It was like going to war for a year, just an experience, and then it's back to normal, walking again with your friends as if it didn't really even happen. But it did. For a time I needed to be in a wheelchair. It wasn't bad. Nothing hurt. It was easy. But it was different, being half as high. When you went up to a bar, you were half as high as everyone else. You looked up to the bartender. It felt more like begging for a drink than ordering one.

Then, one day, at the end of a short vacation on a cruise ship, they had all of us who were in wheelchairs assemble in one large room where we would disembark. The people helping us were so solicitous, so nice, so phony nice, treating us like we were children needing special care. They were speaking down, because we were down; we were lower, lower than they were. I remember the quiet in the room, and this quiet, knowing look that all of us who were lower exchanged, barely moving at all, just the slight glance of eyes exchanged around the room. We all knew what was going on and what we all felt, all of us.

But there was nothing worth saying to them, because we knew they didn't know, they couldn't know how we saw it all. It was our knowing, not theirs, because they couldn't know. They weren't low enough to know. Just like war, the ones that didn't go, they couldn't know. Just "Thank you for your service" now, the token of appreciation; they were so grateful to be able to tell you like they really knew what it was, what it really was for us. They couldn't know what the silence means.

Lawrence Livermore Lab

EDWARD TELLER WAS JUST down the hall from me where I was working in 1983. Just down the hall was the man who figured out the H-bomb, the hydrogen bomb, the one that could have dropped when we were staring down the Russians. It was the bomb that either of us could have dropped, but didn't drop. It would have likely been the end of everything we knew then, of sock hops and drive-ins and expectations for a future, probably the end of us all, all the people on the planet, but maybe not the cockroaches.

Edward Teller was just down the hall at Lawrence Livermore Lab, where they refined and created more efficient bombs, and where I was working for a time. I expected a different kind of place— stern faces, military discipline, guards with machine guns. But they weren't stern, and there were no guards. Instead, there was tai chi on the lawn at lunch hour with the meditative movement of bodies, a serene and soft quiet. The science of bombs was quiet. They were pleasant, the scientists, soft-spoken and serious, like they were doing tai chi. Or maybe that was how you built bombs, like a meditation, the mantra repeating each step of the way.

The scientists were very clear that what they did prevented war, that having the biggest and the most deadly bombs prevented war. They were there to prevent, to protect with an umbrella of retalia-tion, to keep the peace with this umbrella. They were peacemakers, not stern, not warlike. But none of them had ever been on point, on my point, at the edge of annihilation, ready to have their guts strewn over the ground, ready to have their legs and arms blown to hunks of burning meat. I never made that point. That wasn't my job then. But still, I wondered how they'd think if they had been on point.

Vietnam Redux

WHEN THE POLITICAL CONSENSUS began to congeal around going into Iraq and taking Baghdad from Saddam, I saw Vietnam all over again. Some of my ground-pounder, infantry friends saw what I did—that the initial assault would succeed but would not be the end, but the beginning. We knew from our time on the ground that taking one hill does not mean the end of a war. It just incites the guerrilla action that can last and last.

The weapons of mass destruction excuse reminded me of the Gulf of Tonkin, the pivotal aggression that was used as the "instigating reason" for initiating the war in Vietnam. This time, the "instigating reason" was this horrific threat. It didn't matter later that the threat was a paper tiger. There were other "good" reasons by the time the war momentum was well underway. Or was it just that George wanted to finish up where Daddy hadn't, to take Baghdad finally, because Daddy should have done it the first time and it's important to uphold the family name?

I didn't know but I thought it was possible—this lingering family vestige that refocused the data to make it look like this was just the right thing to do. George wasn't in the infantry and hadn't been to war. There was no way he could have really understood, not with that deep down understanding that you get when you take a hill, then leave, then come back and take it again, for no reason other than to take the hill. He'd never taken a hill, watched his buddies get blown to pieces, watched them bleed to death and begin to rot and stink in the sweltering heat.

I knew. I knew it was just the beginning. It reminded me of McNamara and the spreadsheets with the enemy KIAs each week, tallied as blandly as if it were ESPN rattling off the NFL weekly spreads. It was the same, all over again, boys into the bullets, moving across desert terrain to take objectives, cities on a map, like hills in the jungle. It was just the same, the same lack of understanding of what the first assault would provoke, of what the early glory days would turn to. I was watching it all repeat. That's what Al was watching. Only it bothered him more. He had lost his legs. Could Al feel the legs being blown off young boys now—his legs and their legs shattering for some reason that was no reason? Could he feel their pain, the anguish of their families? And then there were the ones who would not return. Maybe he wanted to be with them.

The March to Baghdad

BEFORE THE MARCH TO Baghdad, they decided that this time they were going to take Saddam down. There were arguments for why, justifications for why it was in the national interest, for why there must be a response to Saddam's actions, for why it must be done to save us from the other. It was going to be a fast march to Baghdad to take the city, to take Saddam. Then it would be over in a flash, with the innocent freed in a flash, the oppression halted in a flash, the country freed in a flash, and the war over in a flash. And the arguments for why we were there would be over in a flash.

But my Marine friends and I had been on the ground in a war, a real war, many decades ago. It was a war in the jungle, where battalions could hide in bunkers on the side of a hill, unnoticed from just yards away. In the cities and villages, there were the booby traps, trip wires; it was a war that didn't just go away, go away in a flash. But in a flash this new war seemed to be just like that old war. In a flash it felt too much the same, starting with, the first flash, the dash to Baghdad. The city was a starting point, not an ending point. We knew that this war would not be done in a flash.

We knew there would be more war, a lot more war. Then there would be death, when the war got hot and heavy, with the casualties mounting and a new list of dead soldiers and Marines every day. The news hour would fill with those killed the prior day. We'd hear the silence as their photos and names followed one another. The heroes would return, but not triumphantly—there would be no music, only the silence and the sadness. We knew there would be more war, a lot more war.

But the President and the analysts, sitting in their offices a long way away, had arguments for why it was just, for why it was in the national interest, for why there must be a response to Saddam. But they hadn't been to war, not most of them, probably not any of them on point, on the point squad, on the point fire team, the one Marine at the very front; they hadn't been there. How could they know it would be over, in a flash, after they took Baghdad? But they couldn't know, because they didn't know, that it's not that easy to stop war, stop it in a flash. When you've been on point, you know that war doesn't just stop.

Taking Pfc. Chance

WHEN THE WAR IN Iraq got hot and heavy, I remember that the PBS news hour would start by listing the soldiers and Marines killed the prior day in silence. I could not keep my chest from tightening or keep my eyes dry. I would turn it on each day for a time, to see if I could watch without the emotion overtaking me, but it was always stronger than my will to control it; it was just too hard to do. Then I stopped watching.

But I did watch an HBO special about Marine Lt. Col. Michael Strobl escorting a fallen Marine, shot in Iraq, to his home in Wyoming for burial. In the sequence the airplane captain asks the passengers to remain seated until Pfc. Chance's casket is taken off the plane. As his remains come off the plane, the Colonel is clearly moved by the baggage staff, who stop and line up in observance as the military guard loads the casket into the hearse. I flash back to the time when I was in this same spot, some forty years earlier, as my friend Doug's body was coming off the plane. I feel my chest tightening and hold back the moisture in my eyes. I am back there then, in my mind.

I follow the Colonel to the family's house, but I see myself back with Doug's family. The story of Pfc. Chance has become the story of Doug. It plays over and over for days after. Finally, one day I notice that I have not played the story out in my head. Then I know it is buried again, but I also know the recording is just filed. It can return when it decides, when it is triggered, and when I don't want to see it.

McNamara on Point

I REMEMBER SOMETIME AFTER Dave died when the raging fury had fallen below the boil. It had fallen into a wavelike anger that travelled with me, at my side, just present enough to track me like a shadow, sometimes fading with the night but always returning. It was more obvious when we were on the move—like a shadow I could see it move, because when we were on the move was when the action would most likely happen. And it would most likely happen to the point squad, to the point fire team, to the one Marine at the very front, on the very point.

I wanted McNamara on my point. I wanted the politicians and the generals and the colonels sitting back in Da Nang moving pins on a map—I wanted those bastards on my point. When you're on point, you're marching on the edge of annihilation, your last moment not a full breath away. What is the feeling of your last moment? You don't know that yet, but you might know that any second now.

McNamara was counting KIAs, theirs and ours, like an NFL pick'ems publicizing the point spread each day, clamoring for the numbers, pushing for "probable" numbers of enemy slain to magnify the point spread. It was all about the spread—that was the point. But I wanted him on point, my point, at the edge of annihilation, ready to have his guts strewn over the ground, ready to have his legs and arms blown to hunks of burning meat. I wanted McNamara on point, on my point. That's my point.

He's dead now. I'd like to bring him back. I'd like to put him on point, on my point. And watch him die that way, blown to pieces with just enough time to know what it's like to die that way. That's my point.

Al Leaves Us

I STILL HAVE THE "photograph" in my mind of Al's astonished face as I opened the door at my mother's apartment in Washington D.C. Al didn't realize I was back, and I was astonished to see him leaning on crutches. He had lost both legs, one above and one below the knee. He was there to see my mother, to see how she was doing, thinking I was still in Vietnam. And there he was, standing before me just as positive and upbeat as ever, just without his legs.

I had been thinking about Al. I had been thinking about reconnecting with him. I wanted to see him again at this later stage of life. I knew he had been successful in business for years. Al had an MBA from Stanford to go with his Harvard undergrad degree. Then, later in life, a Bible class turned his life. He had become an Episcopalian minister. Several ministries under his belt led him to Wenatchee, a small town in central Washington. I had been thinking about him when I got the email from a Marine friend with the Wenatchee town newspaper article.

Al was dead. The war in Iraq had made him mad, had brought on the depression that moved in and out of his life. He did not want more young boys to go to war and die. This new war had disturbed him greatly according to those in his flock who knew him well. He found his old .45-caliber pistol and shot himself in the heart. It was a surprise to all who knew him. His wife had just been with him earlier in the day. It was a surprise to her, too. I thought back to the time—Al coming through the apartment door to see my mother, to see how she was doing, only without his legs. I had wanted to see him again. I was surprised. I just wished I had called before. I really wanted to see him again.

Accidental Guerrilla

THERE'S A BOOK CALLED *The Accidental Guerrilla* by David Kilcullen that depicts the endless loop of war we have entangled ourselves in.

The way it works is that the bad guys, the really bad guerrillas wreak havoc on a civilian population. The good guys, like us, go after them but wreak more havoc and civilian casualties. So the locals, who were just trying to live their lives quietly, without any real political leanings for either side—or for any side, because they had never even thought about "sides"—get angry at us, the good guys. So what we have done is turn the locals into guerrillas—either by accident or by stupidity and not understanding the way things will play out.

So the locals who were just trying to live their lives are now guerrillas, terrorists, fighting against us by accident. They become accidental guerrillas, an unthinkable accident, because we were supposed to be fighting for them—not them, not against them. It just happened by accident.

Ho Chi Minh

AFTER HO CHI MINH defeated the French at Dien Bien Phu, we had a choice. We could have lived with Uncle Ho, lived with the fact that he was a communist, lived with this difference and not gone against him, way back then, in 1954. But we went against him, and that was really the start of our war. It was the undeclared war against another commie, part of our new strategy to hold the line against all commies. Because if we didn't, then we believed that democracies would fall like dominoes. And the domino theory became law, to be a commie was treason, and not to fight commies was treason. That's what McCarthy told us.

Uncle Ho didn't plan to take down the U.S. We decided to take him down, over time, bit by bit, until bit by bit didn't work and we had to send in the Marines. Then it wasn't bit by bit anymore. We took bigger and bigger bites. The generals said we could have won if the politicians hadn't let the anti-war protesters have their way, if the politicians had let us stay at it and taken a few more even bigger bites, because we were winning and on our way to victory. Or maybe, maybe even if we had kept going, even then we may have taken on more than we could chew, and it would just have gone on and on—troops still on patrol in the jungles, looking for Gooks to kill, or listening for the trip wire, the subtle snapping sound, the split-second sound that might be the last sound you would ever hear.

Now we're partners with Vietnam. Intel has built a plant there. We visit. They are friendly, like Americans, and love our hi-tech toys and consumer lifestyle. Most are young and weren't even born when the war was on. They have no memory that we were at each other in the villages and jungles, at each other when they were Gooks, whose lives meant nothing next to our own—little soulless, empty carcasses destined for disposal as expeditiously as possible. Now we're partners, friendly, almost friends. We're partners, not enemies, not at war, not at the edge of annihilation and ready to have our guts strewn over the ground, not ready to have our legs and arms blown to hunks of burning meat.

I want to go back to the hills, where we fought at the edge of annihilation, where I can still see the terrain, the craters, the slope of the finger we marched up before enveloping the NVA that had surrounded E Company. I want to go to the spot where Dave died, to be with this space decades later, and to reclaim a feeling. I don't know why, I just know that I want it. I want to reclaim some fragment of the past like there's a moment to find again that has meaning—some remnant I left behind that I need to get back before it's gone. I need to put that piece back inside me, because I'll always be a fragment if I don't.

We Give Them Names

WE CALLED THE NVA and Viet Cong "Gooks." We talked about blowing them away. Sometimes we stacked the bodies up like cordwood and proudly turned in the "confirmed" count up the chain of command to populate McNamara's scorecard. They were just animals in the hunt, skins for the taking. They were the hated, darker-skinned ones, whose lives meant nothing next to our own.

In Iraq and Afghanistan it seems the same. Just now the Gooks have become terrorists. This time the bodies are still counted for each hunting occasion, just rarely totaled and scored the old-fashioned way. McNamara's count was always 'tinkered" with, and no one wants to be associated with the numbers game since Vietnam. It's more complex now. It's harder to quantify "pacification." Did McNamara ever count hearts and minds? I don't think so.

And the terrorists are still little soulless, empty carcasses destined for disposal as expeditiously as possible, whose lives mean nothing next to our own, even if it's some fourteen-year-old trained by his older heroes to be a hero, too, even if there is no way he could possibly know he is a terrorist, not a hero, not doing God's will against the invading enemy, just a little soulless, empty carcass destined for disposal.

But now the Vietnamese are trading partners. They like Americans. They consume like us and want lives like us, with aspirations and families and jobs and even souls. Now they are not the hated, dark-skinned ones—not anymore. But Jane Fonda doesn't get the same deal.

The Taliban terrorists don't get the same deal, either. Their deal is to end up blown away, unless the war ends. Then the deal is over, and time to move on. And after a time, some time, maybe a long time—a decade or so—we'll be trading partners. Mostly they'll like Americans. They already like our hi-tech toys. They'll consume like us and want lives like us, like people we know, not so much the hated terrorists anymore. Still, Jane Fonda doesn't get the same deal.

Mothers at the Front

AFTER BAGHDAD WAS TAKEN and the reality of longer-term, day-to-day combat set in, I would sometimes daydream the impossible. What if every soldier on both sides were required to take their mother with them into battle? And to have their mothers not just in the general area, but mere feet away, just over their left shoulder?

What would happen then? Or what if they had to take their whole family—parents, brothers, and sisters—all surrounding him as they peered over a parapet, staring at the other warrior from the other side. What if the other warrior also had his family crouching around him in the brief instant before the firing would begin?

What then? What would happen? Would it matter? Would the firing start anyway or would they all just stare, hoping for the silence to keep the silence, tensing before a more unimaginable slaughter? But they would be hopeful, yes, hopeful that the presence of the mothers would permeate the air, would penetrate and engulf the politics, the differences, and the righteous retributions. Their presence would permeate all the elements of war that started war but that were not of the present—a soldier staring at another, a human staring at another human, a moment of eyes meeting away from the hurling words of why this all made sense. The sense now was a mother and a son and a mother and a son. There were no words of why the guns were pointed and at the ready, no words of reasons. There would be an empty space, with no words, but fear would lie in the space between them like a layer of fog. There is no contemplation of why it should happen, because the only why, simmering in the fog, is "why?" This is where my daydream ends, in the why and the silent waiting.

Thank You for Your Service

IT'S SO DIFFERENT TODAY when the soldiers come home. Today there are flags and cheers and welcoming rows in the airports when the soldiers come home, like the cheerleaders lining up to make a path for the emerging football team. People wave flags and say, "Thank you for your service." Sometimes today, someone who knows I'm a veteran will say it, say, "Thank you for your service." This happens today, not yesterday, not decades ago when it was better to let your hair grow and just blend back into the civilian population, because if you didn't maybe someone would spit on you and call you names like "baby killer." Back then, no one would say, "Thank you for your service," and there were no cheerleaders lining the ramp off the plane shouting, "Thank you for your service." Don't say that to me now. It's too late. It just makes me angry.

It makes me angry, not because it's late, but because it's way too late. It makes me angry because many of the people proclaiming "Thank you for your service" are making themselves feel good, perhaps even noble because they are heaping praise on the brave warriors today. They feel good because back then, nobody said it, and this makes up for it. These are the proud flag bearers, supporting the troops, saying, "Thank you for your service," pal. And then they get that good, warm feeling inside because "I've supported the troops."

They think that because the troops have been on point, on point for us, we can be proud of them, and then we can be proud ourselves, to have shown how proud we are of them. We can be so proud, almost like it's us—we're going after the terrorists, on point, leading the fight to brave the bullets and incoming, to charge through the smoke and shrapnel, to join the young heroes and blow away the terrorists, whose lives mean nothing next to our own—little, insignificant carcasses destined for a quick disposal.

Fighting for Your Team

WHENEVER THERE'S AN INTERVIEW of one of the troops who has come home or is still there, they say they are fighting for their team, for their buddies on the left and on the right. They are trying to survive and help their buddies survive. Sometimes they say they are proud to fight for their country. But that doesn't come first—they don't talk first about whether the war is just or about preserving democracy. For them and for me, it's about your buddies on your left and on your right, about your team, supporting your team, being there for them, fighting for them, and doing whatever it takes.

Then there's just the silence that lingers like slow moving fog.

They don't talk about the slow moving fog because they know you don't know, don't understand why it's only about your buddies on your left and on your right and about your team. They know you couldn't know what the silence means.

But Not for My Daughter

THERE WILL ALWAYS BE wars. How could anyone think otherwise? Where in time has there been an absence of war? Where in time will there be no anger, no rage, and no sense of injustice. Where in time will there be no violent reaction, no outrage, no vengeance, and no revenge? There will always be wars, and arguments for why, justifications for why, for why it is just, and for why it is in the national interest. There will always be wars.

There will always be anger and road rage and reciprocity. I get angry. I've felt road rage and raced just behind the offender who cut too closely in front of me. And on it goes until we take different turns, and I wonder how the anger burst so suddenly, with the red rage traveling up from my chest to my head. The anger leads to yells and gestures—righteous yells and gestures. Not bullets, but righteous yells and gestures. It doesn't feel right to not retaliate, to let it go quickly.

Letting it go would not be right, except later when the offender is gone, when the red emotion dissipates into the yell, and the yell's reverberations disappear into the sound of the engine and the drone of the traffic. Then I wonder. I wonder—why, why did I, why did I? Now it seems like too much anger, too much for so trivial a cause, not worthy of the cause—not a just cause. There will always be wars.

But not for my daughter. I wouldn't want her to go to war, to any war, to any war for any just cause or certainty of right. I wouldn't want her to go even just to defend from an aggressor with no cause but to harm, to kill. Not for my daughter. How could I see her lost to arguments and justifications for why there must be a response? There will always be wars.

But not for my daughter. I will kill anyone who tries to take her to war. That's my war. That's my rage. That's my justification. There will always be war.

The Dalai Lama

NOT TOO LONG AFTER the war in Iraq started—the second war, George W's war—the Dalai Lama was speaking nearby. He was asked what he would do if someone attacked him. He giggled and said, "Run." There were laughs in the audience. I thought what an interesting response, not to defend and fight, not to roll over and sit quietly for the attacker, but to get away. That wouldn't have been my response. I would have stood my ground and fought back.

Then I wondered what he would do if he were overtaken by the attacker, if he had no chance of escape—what then? But no one asked that next, tougher question. Would he defend and fight or roll over and sit quietly, let the attacker have his way, let the attacker kill him if he wanted, if that was the path? Would he not intervene and not fight back with the courage of the pacifist? I admire his first reaction—to run, to not take offense, to leave the field and not escalate the encounter. But what of the next choice, when running has run out and the last option is fight or die?

Later he was asked what he thought about the war in Iraq. He surprised me. He said it was too early to tell. Even for the Dalai Lama there must be just wars, just killing. Because at some point there may be no place to run and you have to decide whether to roll over and sit quietly for the attacker to have his way, or stand your ground.

War Is a Choice

WAR IS A CHOICE, An ugly choice. It's ugly because once you're engaged, once you're on the ground fighting, it doesn't matter why the choice was made. It doesn't matter whether it was the right choice. It could be a just choice in defense of your homeland, your friends, and your family. Or it could be another kind of choice that sounds more like a strategic political decision—in the national interest, a preemptive taking of a geographic position. It's a strategic move, like a chess game, not so much a just cause, because it's just a game for the politicians.

It's all the same for the guys on the ground. They are trying to survive and help their buddies survive. Sometimes they say they are proud to fight for their country. But that doesn't come first. That's why war is an ugly choice, because even if it is just, it doesn't matter. Or if it is righteous, only as a last resort in defense, surrounded and on the brink of annihilation, it doesn't matter. It doesn't matter if you're on the ground fighting. It doesn't matter because you're going to taste the real thing—the acrid smell of war, the sickening stench of rotting bodies, the wrenching despair when comrades die beside you, the chilling emptiness when your buddies get blown into nothingness, and you're still here. There's nothing to do but wait, hold on, and look out for your buddies, and wait, hold out until you get home, or wait your turn to get blown into nothingness.

That's why if there's a choice, a real choice, then the troops will suffer whether the choice is just or just a chess game. The guys on the ground will suffer either way, unless the choice is not to go. Because they don't have a choice if they go. If they are sent, they don't have a choice about what they will experience. For them, the only choice is to hold on and look out for their buddies, and wait. Hold out until you get home, or wait your turn to get blown into nothingness.

Playing Chess

I REMEMBER MY DI, in a rare philosophical moment, saying that if you were surrounded by the bad guys the sweetest sight you could imagine would be a Marine rifle platoon coming over the ridge to save your ass. That short video plays out for me—the good daydream, the one that makes you proud to have been in a rifle platoon—because if I were surrounded by the bad guys, that's what I would want. I would want to see the sweetest sight you could imagine, a Marine rifle platoon coming over the ridge to save my ass, and to be the safest place you could possibly be—behind a Marine rifle platoon.

That will never change for me—how I feel about the Marines, about the ones I fought with, the ones before me, and especially the ones fighting today. I respect their courage and their strength, the choice they made to be a Marine, the way they take it on. I respect how they charge into whatever they are told to take, take a city, take a life, risk their life, take it all on, run into the bullets, and charge along the edge of eternity. It's not a game, it's life or death; not the game of life or death, just life or death. And all this happens just because they've made that choice—the choice to be a Marine.

But they don't choose where, or when, or whether it's a just cause, or maybe just a chess game. Because it's the politicians in the suits behind their desks who believe it's in our national interest, it will prevent war at our gates, on our soil, in our backyards. So that's the choice, the right choice, just because of that possibility—that makes that choice in our interests, our national interest.

There are many reasons for us being in Iraq and Afghanistan—the strategic cause, to prevent nuclear and biochemical threats, to free the enslaved and bring democracy, and to deny the terrorists a base of operation. There are always reasons and justifications, carefully architected, phrased with precision, and designed to convince even the ones designing the phrases, the stamps of justice, the stamps of assurance, and the stamps of eternal truth. In Vietnam, many reasons and justifications were carefully created—the spread of communism, the domino effect, the Gulf of Tonkin, the SEATO Treaty—obliging us to defend against all that. The march to Baghdad wasn't the end, just the start. Now it was not just the Sunnis running the show anymore, but three tribes—the Shiites and Kurds along with the Sunnis, against each other now, not just us, the war against Saddam, but now the war we ignited between the tribes. And years later, we sit at the edge of conflict with Iran, an Iran that once was forever at odds with Iraq, equalizing the aggressive Iraq of Saddam.

Perhaps in the big chess game we would have been better off letting it be the way it was. How many dead, how many were blasted into nothingness for our national interest? Was it really better for our national interest since along the way we've activated millions more to hate us? We've created accidental guerrillas with a reason to fight, a reason when before there was no reason. It had never occurred to them before, that we were such a demon.

We take Marjah and Kandahar and defend them, for a while, so the citizens can live without fear of war, for a while, so we can bring aid and develop infrastructure and build government and teach them the rule of law, for a while. And for a while there is peace. For a while there is more infrastructure, more peace, until the money dwindles. For a while there is the rule of law, until the troops withdraw, and then it returns—the way it was before, like the tide smoothing out the sand, taking down the sandcastles that were so carefully and thoughtfully constructed. Everything goes back in time, back to the way it was, except not exactly the way it was because now there are more that hate us.

For a while everything we do makes sense, until time passes— just like in Vietnam when we'd take the hill and then leave, the smell of rotting bodies lingering in the bombed-out soil, still pungent, days after the battle. And then we'd leave, leave the hill, empty as it was when it all started, empty like before, except decimated by the fighting. The earth was scorched as if tornadoes had ripped everything to splinters. After time passes you wonder why, why we took that hill. After time passes, it gets harder to understand, harder to see the link, the link between the empty hill and our national interest. It gets harder to see how they connect—the empty hill and the winners and losers of the chess game, and who the winner is. Or is there any winner?

The hill is empty now, just like it was before the war. It was a just war, a war that we had all the reasons for. We had so many reasons for going to take that hill that's empty now before there was all that dying on the hill—the acrid smell, the vomit inducing stench of rotting bodies, the wrenching despair when comrades die, the chilling emptiness that lingers. If you go back to the hill, that chilling emptiness lingers where you remember it, if you go back, go back to where your buddy got blown into nothingness.

Fingers in the Dyke

IT SEEMS THE MORE we fight, the more places we find reason to fight, just or not. The more we fight, the more the number of enemy increases, the more terrorists emerge, and the more places we need to go to suppress their numbers. We feel like we must reduce their capacity to fight and take away the turf that they own, so they don't have a place to fight from, a sanctuary, a base, a home base. But they fight, withdraw from our might, disappear into the mountains or the villages, and then emerge again, like putting fingers in the dyke.

And if they don't surface in another country, or back in the same spot we fought before, then they—or someone just like them, sometimes even just like us, or one of us—emerge downtown, just down the road, in my neighborhood. Because there's no place where you can fence it off and keep out the bad guys. There's no place where you can build a castle, with a moat and thick walls that resist penetration; there's no place safe, no place like home anymore, because home isn't safe anymore.

So we fight on, take away their bases, for a while, take away their sanctuary, for a while, and blow away as many bad guys as we can along the way. But their numbers seem to grow; one step forward, two steps back—one terrorist killed, two more are born. We create two more accidental guerrillas for every one we take out. How would McNamara score this chess game? Only count the ones taken out, or count both and see the body toll in reverse, more created than eliminated? He would probably just count the ones taken out. That looks better.

How you keep score is how it's all presented—regardless of what type of choice it was. It's all just a game, just a game for the politicians to keep score, their score, their way. It doesn't matter though, not if you're on the ground. It doesn't matter if you're on the ground, running to the bullets, putting fingers in the dyke day after day.

There Will Always Be War

THERE WILL ALWAYS BE bad guys, the ones who will make war just because there will always be a reason. There will always be a need for revenge, a need to defend, and a need in the national interest. There will always be a political advantage through a game of global chess to be played out mostly by young men, played out with collateral damage, mostly to civilians, children, and to those not even understanding the why, or just accepting the why their leaders provide because that's the only why they know. And people will always fight to stay alive, with their backs against the wall. That's the only choice—not much of a choice, just the natural reaction to stay alive, not so much a choice as a reaction, like raising your arms as someone is about to strike you.

But sometimes, lots of the time, maybe most of the time, there's a choice. We know there's a choice because there's a debate about the choice, debate before the choice is made, before the gathering momentum defines the reasons for war. Too often the stamps of eternal truth coalesce as the debate, and the choices, the reasons to go to war engulf all the reasons not to. But what if you could go forward in time, to the time when it was all over, when we were back to being friends, even allies? What if we could go forward in time and see when we were not fighting, not angry, not killing, but working together on the same team? What if we could go forward in time and see all this, see it all before we make the choice now, see how it will be before we decide to go to war? Then would we still go to war anyway, because if we didn't it wouldn't end up in the future this way, because we had to fight to maintain our national interest?

If I were in Hanoi today, would I be able to see the young 14-year-old NVA soldier, now nearly my age, and shake his hand instead of just remembering his limp, silent, young body? Did I have to look at the photograph of him with his family around their dining room table just above his limp, silent, young body? Or could it have been different if a different choice were made, if the reasons not to go to war had countered the reasons for going to war? There would have been a difference for me—what I would have never known, never learned. I would have never learned about war.

But what if I could have gone forward in time, to the time when it was all over, when we were back to being friends? How would I decide at that moment before war, before my war? Would I decide still to go to war?

Twins

I FEEL LIKE THERE are two sides of me—like twins joined together, in different places sometimes, left- and right-handed, sometimes at the hip, but sometimes I just feel like one twin, one side. At the beginning, before the war, my war, I carried the image of John Wayne charging into the bullets, up the hill, always victorious, the music carrying the hero each lurching step along the way to accomplish the mission, save the fallen, and savor the battle. And then, there was the triumphal return, the admiration, the glory, and the hero's inner glow. At the beginning, there was just one twin, just the charge, just the reward, the inner glow, the full chest, the special feeling that sets heroes a step beyond the rest.

Then the war, when Dave died, brought out the other side, the other twin. The angry me became all I knew. Then I came back and forgot both sides, forgot it all. I just looked at the future, no war in my face, like college was over and it was time to move on and move forward to the next life beyond all that. The war was not all forgotten, but it was all in the past, all in the back of my mind; it was out of everyday mind, most of the time.

But decades later, when the swift march to Baghdad was on, I saw John Wayne again charging into the bullets, up the hill to savor the hero's glory. I watched John Wayne, and then became John Wayne. I wanted to get the call, to return to the march, to brave the bullets and incoming. I wanted to charge through the smoke and shrapnel and to join the young heroes, and blow away the terrorists. The first side of me, the first twin, had returned.

Then there was death, the list of dead soldiers and Marines every day on the news hour. I would turn it on each day for a time, to see if I could watch without the emotion overtaking me, stronger than my will to control it. It was just too hard to do. Then I stopped watching, before the anger could simmer through the mist, before the other side, the other twin could overtake the first, and would bury John Wayne.

But now they were both in the room, moving at different times across the stage, sometimes one, then the other, all in the back of my mind, out of everyday mind, most of the time.

The Warrior's Silence

WHEN I WAS A Young teenager learning to play the guitar in the late fifties, I'd strum along to the *Kingston Trio* albums. I don't remember having a favorite, but I do remember one song. I remember the words; they come back to me now and then: "Where have all the flowers gone, gone to graveyards every one, when will they ever learn, when will they ever learn."

I've seen the flowers and the graveyards that I imagined then. I see real graves, for friends fallen, for Marines who are in those graveyards. I know this song differently than when I was a young teenager, but it still leaves me with the same feeling—the quiet, the silence that was inside the song. It's a song of silence inside the emptiness. It's about something lost, something that's fallen into the emptiness that didn't have to be lost. I understand now, in the silence, where the flowers have gone—gone to graveyards, graveyards I have been to. I heard the silence then, way back then. I heard the silence, felt the emptiness, the fall into the hollow, the hollow that sucks it all out of you, all of what you thought you were—sucks it all the way down, down this hollow drain, into the emptiness.

When someone asks me about the Vietnam War, about any war, I feel the silence envelop me. I don't want to talk, because talk is not about the war. The silence is about the war, but they wouldn't understand, couldn't understand, if they hadn't been to war. They wouldn't understand that talking about war doesn't capture what it does, what it takes away. It takes away something inside, something you can't get back, because there's just that silence, the emptiness. I can feel the silence with other veterans, veterans of war, of any war—the quiet knowing, and knowing that you can't talk about it because talking about it, isn't it. We speak the silence, the shared understanding of the emptiness, because the emptiness can be understood by those that know it. The emptiness replaces something lost, that didn't have to be lost, but was lost, that's been replaced, replaced by the silence. The silence bears witness.

About the Author

Ord Elliott was a Marine Rifle Platoon Commander in Vietnam in 1967. He went on to build a successful career in management consulting. He is the author of a book on organization design, *The Future Is Fluid Form: Practical Steps for Designing Flat, Flexible Organizations.* He lives in Woodside, California.